TRANSFORMING TROUBLED CHILDREN, TEENS, AND THEIR FAMILIES

In *Transforming Troubled Children, Teens, and Their Families: An Internal Family Systems Model for Healing,* Dr. Mones presents the first comprehensive application of the Internal Family Systems (IFS) Therapy Model for work with youngsters and their families. This model centers diagnosis and treatment around the concept of the Functional Hypothesis, which views symptoms as adaptive and survival-based when viewed in multiple contexts. The book provides a map to help clinicians understand a child's problems amidst the reactivity of parents and siblings and to formulate effective treatment strategies that flow directly from this understanding. This is a non-pathologizing systems and contextual approach that brings out the natural healing capacity within clients. Dr. Mones also shows how a therapist can open the emotional system of a family so that parents can let go of their agendas with their children and interact in a loving, healthy, and Self-led way.

This integrative MetaModel combines wisdom from psychodynamic, structural, Bowenian, strategic, sensorimotor, and solution-focused models with IFS Therapy. A glossary of terms is provided to help readers with concepts unique to IFS. Unique to this approach is the emphasis on shifting back and forth between intrapsychic and relational levels of experience. Therapy vignettes are explored to help therapists address issues such as trauma, anxiety, depression, somatization, and oppositional and self-destructive behavior in children, along with undercurrents of attachment injury. Two detailed cases are followed over a full course of treatment. A section on frequently asked questions explores work with families of separation and divorce, resistance, the trajectory of treatment, dealing with anger, the linking to twelve-step programs, and much more. This is an ideal book for any therapist in quest of understanding the essence of healing and seeking therapeutic strategies applied within a compassionate framework.

Arthur G. Mones, PhD, ABPP, is a Diplomate in Clinical Psychology and Faculty in the Postgraduate Program in Couple Therapy at the Derner Institute, Adelphi University. He is an AAMFT Approved Supervisor and a Certified IFS Therapist. Dr. Mones maintains a practice in Hewlett, Long Island in New York, specializing in individual, couple, and family therapy, and offers workshops and consultation groups to professionals of all disciplines.

TRANSFORMING TROUBLED CHILDREN, TEENS, AND THEIR FAMILIES

An Internal Family Systems Model for Healing

Arthur G. Mones

Routledge
Taylor & Francis Group

NEW YORK AND LONDON

First published 2014
by Routledge
711 Third Avenue, New York, NY 10017

and by Routledge
27 Church Road, Hove, East Sussex BN3 2FA

Routledge is an imprint of the Taylor & Francis Group, an informa business

© 2014 Taylor & Francis

Library of Congress Cataloging-in-Publication Data
Mones, Arthur G.
  Transforming troubled children, teens, and their families : an internal
family systems model for healing / Arthur G. Mones. — 1 Edition.
  RC489.F33M66 2014
  616.89′140835—dc23
  2013050995

ISBN: 978-0-415-74421-8 (hbk)
ISBN: 978-0-415-74423-2 (pbk)
ISBN: 978-1-315-81313-4 (ebk)

Typeset in Sabon
by Apex CoVantage, LLC

Printed and bound in the United States of America by Publishers Graphics,
LLC on sustainably sourced paper.

This book is dedicated to the memory of my parents, David and Kelly Mones. Thank you for teaching me about family. Your protection and acceptance gave me room to grow and think on my own.

To my wife, Leslie, my daughter, Lara, and my son, Masa. I am proud of our how our family seeks to bring goodness, creativity, and compassion to each other and to the world. In some small way, we try to make a difference. Your love is my home base.

CONTENTS

CONTENTS

FOREWORD

I am very honored by this book and very happy to write this foreword. This work represents an important expansion of the literature on Internal Family Systems (IFS) psychotherapy, providing a practical framework and methodology for working with families and children.

This is also an advance in the field of family therapy. I was around for those thrilling years in the 1970s when the pioneers of family therapy created their separate schools of thought, and I have been influenced by each of them. They were reacting to the acontextual, individual focus of psychoanalysis that ignored the family, and as such made little effort to incorporate a map of the mind into their systemic view. Their sense was that understanding families was complicated enough, and that adding the intrapsychic level would make models overwhelmingly complex. The family therapy pioneers believed that emotional healing would occur as external family relationships improved.

As it became clear that models of family therapy that only considered the external layer of systems were inadequate, there were attempts to fit various forms of neo-Freudian intrapsychic models into existing family frameworks. Those never caught on because the concepts of such models were not based in systems theory and, consequently, contradicted the non-pathologizing and contextual understanding that family therapy had ushered in.

Because I was steeped in systems thinking, when clients began describing their inner experience to me as composed of different parts of them that had conflicts in their minds, I applied the same concepts and techniques to what seemed to be an inner family, which had been useful working on the interpersonal level. As a result, IFS is systems-based, and as such integrates easily with various family therapies. Also, the compassionate, resourceful Self that I found at the core of clients fits well with the focus on promoting strengths and fostering optimism, as emphasized by the family systems models.

I, however, began working increasingly with individual adults rather than families so as to fully explore the inner landscape and possibilities for healing at that level. Thus, I'm extremely grateful for Art and other therapists who have spent many of those same years applying IFS to children and families and who are now writing about it in a clear and compelling way. Art was an accomplished family therapist when he came to IFS and now draws on decades of experience using IFS with troubled children and their families.

Thus, this book brings a model to the field of family therapy that enables therapists to shift their foci in both the assessment and treatment phases—from the family to the intrapsychic levels and back—smoothly and with consistent and parallel assumptions and methods. Therapists can now not only restructure family relationships and improve communication, but also help family members identify and transform the inner parts that keep their reactions to one another extreme, as well as help family members be able to communicate to one another about those parts from a state of Self-leadership.

In addition to innovating in those ways, this book is comprehensive, including practical and sage advice on a wide variety of topics, from how to conduct the first phone call with a family member, to whom to include when in session, to how to use IFS in play therapy with a child. In addition, several key topics are included, such as Self-led parenting, using IFS with teens, and applications with younger kids. Finally, several detailed case illustrations bring these concepts to life and help the reader realize that it can be a fascinating and empowering process for clients and therapists.

Now when workshop participants or family therapy colleagues ask me how IFS applies to working with families and children, it is a big relief that I can point them to this excellent book.

Richard C. Schwartz, PhD

ACKNOWLEDGMENTS

I feel fortunate to have found psychology. I believe in the goodness of human beings and their tenacious mechanisms of survival in navigating obstacles and trauma. I am honored to be in a career that brings out Self-energy in me that can extend to the healing process of others. Learning is challenging and comforting at the same time. Each new bit of knowledge generates new questions. I like this about life and enjoy participating in this process. Some of the ideas and therapeutic strategies explored in this book will challenge you, and some will comfort you. My hope is that this experience will stretch your thinking and deepen your work.

On these pages, I acknowledge how I learned what I learned so that I can bring the ideas in this book to you.

Without knowing it, I became a family therapist in my family of origin. My parents created a child-focused family, and were consistent cheerleaders who fostered room for finding out what my strengths might be. They were a model of a devoted couple that loved kids. As first-generation Americans, they were filled with hope accompanied by anxiety about how to make their way. My challenges and questioning of authority were accepted. I was accepted. While I made them exasperated at times, they wanted me to go beyond their limitations. I thank them for this gift. My older brother, Dr. Richard Mones, kept me on my toes at all times, with a constant barrage of humor that ranged from the silly to high sophistication. He introduced me to jazz and to a love of science. It is no accident that we both specialize in work with kids, he a pediatrician and I a psychologist. To this day, we share an awe of evolution and its powerful influences in every area of life. His loyalty and support, then and now, are greatly appreciated. We all struggled in various ways with what to do with our vulnerability as we traversed an unpredictable world that, for us, included illness, loss, and extended family members struggling to grow, differentiate, and launch from powerful enmeshment. I made that human struggle into a career.

I attended Public School 97 in Bensonhurst, Brooklyn, where my talents in writing were recognized and cultivated by dedicated teachers who fostered learning in a climate of encouragement and respect. I began playing trumpet at ten years old, which, I learned, allowed feelings inside to be expressed. I played baseball in every form on the streets of my neighborhood and could reach "a couple of sewers" in stickball. Our parents introduced us to the movies and theatre. I had lots of friends along the way and have fond memories of laughing hysterically at the back of the classroom, to the consternation of my teachers, who mostly accepted me and only rarely punished my rude behavior. There were many losses of relatives early on, leading me to question why bad things happen to good people and contributing to the formation of my belief system that looks mostly inward in grappling with such questions. In Bensonhurst Junior High School and Lafayette High School I enjoyed studying science and literature, again with very talented teachers. In those years, Shakespeare grabbed me with his insights into life, while evolution challenged me with its map of life that leads to insights.

I took a required course in Psychology at Brooklyn College in 1968 after my sophomore year. I was hooked. Beginning to learn about the inner workings of humanity coincided with the social upheaval of those times. I was proud to be introduced to a field that grapples with individual and societal struggle. My professors were open minded and progressive thinkers. I continued my learning and received my doctorate from Long Island University, Brooklyn Center. I discovered that I sought the big picture—to understand what the essence is in the psychotherapeutic process and to see the Common Factors among the various models then being presented (psychoanalytic and behavioral).

My learning in clinical psychology was quickly linked to my interest in working with kids, as I had served as counselor to developmentally challenged children in special education camps and programs in California and New York during my summers as a young adult. As I completed my training, I was drawn to learn about family therapy, again needing to see the bigger picture and to work on a larger canvas. This was a very powerful eye opener that initiated my thinking about symptoms as survival strategies within the family context. My clinical supervisors, to their credit, prodded my quirky thinking, and some were able to steer me toward a wondrous world of talented and groundbreaking personalities.

My "guru" search began. From my readings of Gregory Bateson and with a strong link to Darwin's theory of evolution, I met with, was supervised by, took courses from, read books and articles by, and watched hours of videotaped sessions of an amazing array of therapists: Milton Erickson, Richard Bandler, John Grinder, Jay Haley, Virginia Satir, Salvador Minuchin, Murray Bowen, Paul Watzlawick, Betty Carter, Peggy Papp, Phil Guerin, Tom Fogarty, Carl Whitaker, Cloe Madanes, Harry Aponte, and others. The common ingredient of these master therapists? Courage to break the mold and to take on the most challenging cases. This remains an inspiration.

As I learned, I worked with clients, first during an internship at Nassau County Medical Center on Long Island, then at the Astor Child Guidance Clinics in Poughkepsie and Rhinebeck, New York, and at Peninsula Counseling Center in Woodmere, New York. Alongside my direct service hours, I became a clinical supervisor, administrator, and researcher. I spent time writing about some of my own ideas. I developed a private practice on Long Island. I served as Coordinator of the Specialization in Family and Couples Therapy in the doctoral program in clinical psychology at St. John's University. We established a postgraduate program at the same school. I served as Faculty and Clinical Supervisor in the Family Therapy Program at the Long Island Institute for Psychoanalysis and Psychotherapy. I am currently on faculty in the postgraduate program in Couple Therapy at the Derner Institute at Adelphi University.

I very frequently attended the annual Psychotherapy Networker meetings in Washington, DC. Here, there was exposure to the best and brightest of the clinical field. The meetings themselves provided (and continue to do so) a four-day congregation of excitement as thousands of therapists gathered to learn cutting-edge ideas, presided over by Dr. Richard Simon. In these meetings during the 1980s, I met Dick Schwartz, PhD, and learned about his new model, Internal Family Systems Therapy. I continued to learn from Dick through his writings and workshops, in direct supervision and later in formalized training. Here it was, a model that articulated and operationalized what I was striving to formulate—a non-pathologizing way of looking at human beings, a way to understand the survival-based, protective nature of psychological symptoms in the service of dealing with human suffering. It was family therapy turned inside and out.

Dick also exuded what the other masters did—courage to work confidently with very challenging people. Here was a person and a model who captured human nature as closely as I had experienced.

My own closer circle needs to be mentioned: teachers, friends, and colleagues who have influenced and supported my growth as a psychologist: John Exner, Gustav Gilbert, Elizabeth Van Laer, Stuart Pace, Aaron Balasny, Ruth Stark, Ephraim Biblow, Bruce Bernstein, Robert Katz, Ed Reese, Arthur Phillips, Theresa Donnelly, Constance Flood, Jerry Kleiman, Robert Sherman, Robert Eakin, Herbert Ruben, Alvin Balaban, Gisa Indenbaum, Linda Klein Lenkowsky, Steven Krantz, Jenny Heinz, Peggy Neimeth, Carl Bagnini, Ralph Cohen, Susan McConnell, Pamela Krause, Michi Rose, Stanford Griffith, Louis Primavera, Rafael Javier, and Michael Zentman. Special thanks goes to Rabbis Lee Friedlander and Joy Levitt, who have helped me shape questions of faith and belief in very meaningful ways. Very special appreciation goes to our dear friends Linda and Steve Einsidler, for being there for us even when we didn't know we needed you.

My appreciation to Marian Sandmaier for reviewing an early draft of this book. Special thanks goes to Dick Schwartz for reading and making important suggestions in response to the early draft. I am deeply honored and grateful that Dick provided the foreword to this book.

The not-so-secret secret is that teaching and supervision have provided a wonderful challenge and opportunity to "get it right." I continue to learn tremendously from this process and I am greatly indebted to my students for their openness to present their questions and struggles. And just when I think I understand the essence of it all, along comes another challenge: an individual or family that have me questioning this knowledge once again. My thinking continues to evolve; my therapy extends to novel approaches.

Finally, and most importantly: my family. Out of all my life accomplishments, I am most proud of being a husband and father. I know that these are my most important roles, and I am blessed to have Dr. Leslie Taynor as a wonderful life partner, sharing in a rich, meaningful journey together, celebrating joyous life events, and supporting each other through the inevitable times of disappointment, loss, and struggle. Her encouragement and belief in me helped to make my continuing growth possible and, among other life accomplishments, helped to bring about this book. It is has been the greatest joy to see Lara grow from a cute, enthusiastic kid to an adult who is making her mark in the specialty area of Japanese Performing Arts. It is a special treat to peek in on her life, as others value her opinions and are appreciative recipients of her knowledge, generous kindness, and caring. Leslie and I feel fortunate to have welcomed Masa, professor at Middlebury College, into our family as our new son, who creates safety and comfort to Lara (and us) with his compassionate view of life and who expands our lives to Eastern beliefs and sensibilities. We try hard to not get in their way so that they can fully blossom. I carry rich memories and wisdom of my in-laws, Dr. Irving Taynor and Lillian Taynor as models of deep devotion to family and commitment to the repair of the world.

I have been fortunate to have been found by Routledge Publishers. Shortly after submitting my work for consideration, I had the privilege to meet, via email, Marta Moldvai, Associate Editor. Marta immediately "got" this MetaModel and could see its potency and potential. She has guided the process of bringing this book to fruition with great professionalism and in a manner that frequently quelled my anxious Parts. Elizabeth Lotto, Editorial Assistant, was also invaluable in bringing her skills to shape the final product. The niceness, kindness, and steadiness were tremendously helpful.

There are many more to be recognized, as, along the way, you brought your Self-energy to me when it was needed. I call you my angels. You appeared, touched my life, and made it stronger. I learned from that.

Thank you. All of you.

Part One

THE INTERNAL FAMILY SYSTEMS METAMODEL

1

THE ESSENCE OF EMOTIONAL HEALING

I assume that each person who enters my treatment office is seeking psychological healing. Each child, each parent, and each sibling carries emotional burdens and seeks relief from sadness, fear, shame, and feelings of inadequacy. Yes, even those children who protest being there, parents who say that they are too busy to participate, or kids who externalize the blame onto other family members are looking to be healed. Even those who are developmentally disabled and unable to represent their thoughts in easily discernible ways seek healing. All who enter seek to release emotional pain and to bring their Self-energy to both their inner and relational worlds.

Psychotherapy is a very powerful process. This book is about deep emotional healing for children and their families through applying a MetaModel, the Internal Family Systems (IFS) Model to children, their parents, and siblings. I will put forward a way of thinking, a conceptual map, to guide the clinician who works with child-focused problems. This conceptual map will be enhanced by presenting therapeutic applications of the IFS MetaModel.

The essence of psychological healing with children is to depathologize them. These children are referred to us by parents, teachers, pediatricians, and the legal system. We are expected to treat their "problems"—defiance, aggression, depression, anxiety, peer difficulties, addictions, somatization, etc., as would a medical practitioner treat a virus or a broken leg. The child has not asked to come to our office. A person in authority, usually a parent, has brought the child to us to be "fixed." Often, by the time a child has come to see us, he has been referred for psychological or educational evaluations, special education, medical workups, and so on, resulting in feelings of being inadequate, "bad," a disappointment to his parents, a problem in the classroom, ostracized by peers, and so on.

We will need to see potential where hopelessness has set in. We will need to see goodness when those connected to the child view him as a "problem." We will need to see strengths. Most of all, we will need to understand that his symptoms are attempts at psychological survival. Whether the child is aggressive or withdrawn, internalizing or externalizing, noncompliant or pseudomature, we will need to put his symptoms in context—family, school, neighborhood, and internal emotional environment—and see that he is trying to cope with trauma, from mild to severe, resulting in insecure Attachment, anxiety, sadness, shame, and feelings of inadequacy.

Instead of a medically oriented diagnosis, the centerpiece of this model will be **The Functional Hypothesis: childhood symptomatology is an attempt by the child to cope within a context that is emotionally traumatizing. The symptoms are attempts at psychological survival. These survival strategies work in the short run, but when overemployed will generate new problems that make life even more difficult for the child and family.**

Ana, age six, was referred to me because of frequent tantrums with her mother. In my initial consultation meeting with her mother, Blanche, I learned that the parents had been divorced for two years, following a tumultuous history that included the father's severe alcohol binges and physical abuse of Blanche, witnessed by Ana. The father's second marriage is on shaky ground. Ana's stepmother is a supportive figure. Currently, the father is in jail, awaiting trial for assault and robbery. Blanche's father died several years ago from complications of alcoholism. Her mother has become frail in recent years. Blanche is working full time, requiring child care and after-school programs for Ana. Blanche looked exhausted. She expressed her concerns for Ana in a very loving manner. She wanted me to reduce Ana's tantrums.

I told her I was hopeful that in a collaborative therapy with her and Ana, we would do this. When I asked her whether she would want help in not becoming so frustrated and powerless in her parenting, she replied warily, "I don't know if that would be possible, but I'd like your help with that."

Next I met Ana and her mother together. Ana made an immediate connection to me. Some confusion on her face about coming to a therapist dissolved into relief as I asked and learned about her strengths—she is smart, verbal, artistic, and strong-willed. She was trying very hard to show me that she is happy, however, her face looked tired and sad. When I gently asked about mother-daughter issues, Ana volunteered that she has frequent "hissy fits" when her mother says no to her demands. I continued my assessment sessions with more time with Ana and Blanche and Ana alone, and then a followed up with a parent-feedback session with Blanche.

The Diagnosis? Oppositional Defiant Disorder, According to our DSM Categories

My diagnosis: a child trying hard to Manage day to day, who lets loose her frustration when her mother, pressured and Managerial herself, breaks their connection while disciplining. Both are sad, tired, and longing for soothing. Ana's tantrums are self-preservative—"You can't control me!" ("I am my own person, and I will be in charge of how close and how far we are emotionally.") The fight buffers an underlying sadness and loss. The Functional Hypothesis states that symptoms are coping mechanisms. When Ana and Blanche sit in my office, I see this clearly.

When a child is referred for psychotherapy, she has been labeled as a "problem." Problem children come in two general clusters: externalizing symptoms, such as defiant behavior, being socially challenging or aggressive, addictions of alcohol and drugs, or internalizing symptoms, such as anxiety, obsessions, compulsions, depression, and somatic complaints. The tendency is to label and try to remove the symptoms. This is consistent with the Medical Model that is prevalent in our society. The Medical Model will bring in "experts" to "cure" the child—usually by means of medication, psychological testing, educational evaluations, special education, tutors, etc., all with good intentions, to help. Unless this is done in a very careful, humanistic context, the treatment offerings will alienate the child and have her believe that she is "damaged goods" and not accepted as is. This process of pathologizing the child can lead to a lifetime of marginalization. Rather than lead to a "cure," this form of treatment can deepen the already perplexing problems faced by parents and educators. Even when symptoms abate, damage will have occurred via over-management and coercion of the youngster.

In contrast, the MetaModel is a depathologizing model. It assumes that symptoms are adaptational strategies for survival. When a child is defiant, he is expressing an attempt to cope with painful feelings and relational constraints. Parents are often feeling extremely agitated and powerless. They, too, are attempting to cope with painful feelings and relational constraints when viewed in context. In this book we will explore how the MetaModel places child symptoms in context to understand their functional nature, and how to generate treatment strategies that are accepting and depathologizing. With the MetaModel, the therapist will engage the child and family in a collaborative experiential process that links to the self-curative aspects that each human being possesses.

The MetaModel used in this book will be based on Internal Family Systems Therapy (IFS) as developed by Richard C. Schwartz, PhD. It is my belief that IFS is the most effective MetaModel in bringing out the clients' strengths in a humanistic manner. The IFS approach is most consonant to human nature and is a comprehensive, deeply healing model. IFS will be introduced below and will serve as our vocabulary for the MetaModel of healing as well as the process of therapeutic intervention. The MetaModel is consistent with the Common Factors Model (Hubble, Duncan & Miller, 1999; Duncan, Miller, Wampold & Hubble, 2010),

Contextual Model (Wampold, 2001), and Second-Order Change Model (Fraser & Solovey, 2007), models that have the most potent empirical support for emotional healing. Here we apply these principles to the treatment of troubled children and their families.

It will be useful to address the issue of evidence-based treatment from the outset. Evidence-based treatment is founded in testing scientific hypotheses via empirical findings scrutinized through the lens of double-blind randomized trials. This is known as the Medical Model. The complexity of this process for psychotherapy is explored and clarified by Wampold (2010). The field of psychotherapy has tried to align itself with the medical model in the hopes of legitimizing itself and establishing guidelines for applying specific approaches for particular disorders. When rigorous studies are performed, it turns out that "a variety of treatments, when administered by therapists who believe in the treatment and when accepted by the clients, are equally effective . . . there is little evidence that the specific ingredients of any treatment are responsible for the benefits of therapy" (Wampold, 2010, p. 71). The statistical differences that are discovered are due to the qualities of the therapist-patient relationship that can bring out the healing capacity of the clients. These qualities are called "Common Factors."

Will Internal Family Systems Therapy just turn out to be another approach that is as good or as limited as all the others? My opinion is that IFS is on a meta-level, consistent with the Contextual Model Common Factors of the therapist-client alliance that is able to access client factors for emotional healing. It is a model that lifts constraints from natural healing processes of the client, akin to releasing the curative nature of the person's autoimmune system, which staves off intrusive germs and is able to repair injuries that inevitably occur in life. In addition, there is a qualitative difference in the study of the psychological/emotional sphere of human nature and the study of isolated biological systems. Therapists are more like naturalists studying cultures and tribes than laboratory investigators (Bateson, 1972; Haley, 1981). The former, for success to occur, need to invite in every detail and dynamic, whether neat or messy, clear or confusing. On the other hand, laboratory scientist needs to "control" the experiment by ruling out any extraneous factors that may contaminate the matter being studied. It is important to note that the field of contextual theory that became the family systems therapy field was begun by Gregory Bateson, who was a naturalist and ethnologist, married to Margaret Mead, an anthropologist. Bateson and colleagues were the first to study families of schizophrenic patients by having two therapists in the room with the family and the rest of the team placed behind a one-way mirror to study the pattern of communications. This would be similar to the participant-observer model in naturalistic investigations. It is my contention, then, that therapists are immersed in "field studies" and our "data" is wide ranging. According to the Common Factors Model, the placebo effect, so crucial to "control" in the Medical Model, has actually turned out to be, in large part, the healing aspects in the psychotherapy contextual model, i.e., it is not the specific technique applied but the cultivation of a healing therapist-patient relationship that will bring forth the natural ability of the patient to repair psychological trauma.

The Internal Family Systems MetaModel is summarized below and woven throughout this book as a way to further understand and clarify how healing occurs, both as a road map for the therapist and as the operational vehicle for making the healing occur (Schwartz 1995, 2001; Schwartz & Goulding 1995).

IFS is a model that elucidates the themes of family therapy and extends the work to the internal, intrapsychic world of the client. IFS views the internal psychological world of human beings as made up of an ecological system of Parts or subpersonalities. The choreography of the Parts is consistent with the models of family systems therapy as applied in the relational sphere. At the center of the internal system is the core Self that holds and expresses the compassion, courage, curiosity, clarity, confidence, creativity, calm, and ability to connect to others. According to the apocryphal story, an admirer asked Michelangelo how he was able to create the magnificent sculpture of David from a solid block of marble. Michelangelo replied, "David was in there all along, I just knew how to bring him forth." In other words, the Self is that good, healing energy that the therapy process "brings forth" when it is successful. These attributes of Self are consistent with Eastern philosophy and teachings, and the focus on self-efficacy and self-acceptance are woven throughout the more recent conversation about Common Factors.

Here, Self is our basic pure human nature that we possess from birth. It is the pure "David" who lives in the block of marble, waiting for a gifted artist to bring out. For all of us to some degree, this healing energy of Self is blocked as a result of traumatic emotional experiences, imperfect caretaking, and existential anxiety (Becker, 1973). As a result, we carry sadness, fear, shame, and emotional pain that is not fully metabolized because we were too young and ill equipped to process it and because parents were not fully available and not fully capable in helping us through these experiences, due to their own constraints on Self-energy. The residue of this emotional pain is labeled Exiles in this model. For our survival, the full experience of Exiles is felt to be too overwhelming, so they are compartmentalized and guarded at all costs.

In order to help accomplish this banishment of emotional pain, two sets of other Parts are activated. One category is called the Managers. These Parts emphasize internal and interpersonal control and do all that they can to keep the "gate" locked so that the person does not go too close to the experience of painful Exiles. The Managers protect the Self from this pain (functional hypothesis/survival strategy) but in the process create new difficulties and limit the healthy range of being in Self, intrapsychically and relationally.

On the other end of the spectrum, is another set of protective Parts, called Firefighters. These Parts serve the same purpose as Managers, i.e., to protect the emotional pain from overwhelming the person. Firefighters act to soothe and distract from this pain (functional hypothesis/survival strategy). The most common Firefighters are addictions of all sorts, providing a "quick fix" analgesic to the long-held residue of trauma. As Managers and Firefighters are called into service of blocking intrapsychic pain, the energy and qualities of Self are eclipsed. As Self is constrained, defensive and self-protective survival strategies (i.e., Managers and Firefighters) play a dominant role in our internal emotional system and interpersonal relational experience, and who we are (our identity) begins to resemble these defensive parts and not our compassionate, competent Selves. So, consistent with our central theme, the solutions in the service of protection of our emotional system, when overworked, will create new constraints on our mental health.

The therapeutic process in IFS is to help guide the Self back to its rightful leadership position within the internal system through safe, experiential exploration. First, protective Managers and Firefighters need to be differentiated and unblended from Self. Recognition of the positive intentions of these Parts—their protection of the person—is a central part of this process and a direct application of the Functional Hypothesis. Once the Self-energy is liberated, the next phase of treatment consists of unburdening the Exiles so that there are new degrees of emotional freedom throughout the internal system.

The IFS Model places great emphasis on the process of unburdening the remnants of trauma held by the Exiled Parts. It is necessary but not sufficient to apply the Functional Hypothesis without having the Self of the client *experiencing* the emotional pain as the client and the therapist bear witness to this experience. Without this deep emotional process, the client will not be fully free from the effects of past trauma and will predictably become re-traumatized from intrapsychic and/or interpersonal triggers that are embedded in body memory (Pert, 1997; Rothschild, 2000; Ogden et al., 2006). This is consistent with an ecological (systems) model. As the Functional Hypothesis is applied so that the Self is in a leadership position, Protective Parts will become activated, vigilant in their attempts to buffer the surfacing of pain. Ultimately, this pain seeks expression and needs healing and unburdening. Clients often choose to create a ritual through which to unburden deeply held emotional pain. This is consistent with Garfield (1992), who views therapeutic rituals linked to reattribution as a meta-level process in all therapy models. Changes in the internal emotional system can powerfully affect changes in the external system (child's family). Working on both levels will be crucial in this model, as will be demonstrated throughout this book.

In the chapters ahead, we will learn how to understand the world of children using the Internal Family Systems MetaModel and how to apply the essence of psychological healing.

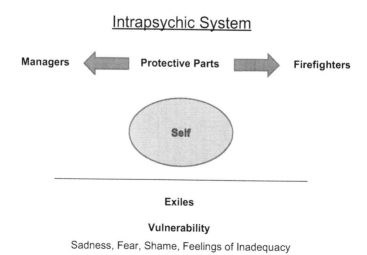

Figure 1.1 Intrapsychic System

Glossary of Terms for the Internal Family Systems MetaModel

The following list of terms that articulate the Internal Family Systems MetaModel are offered to readers as an aid to familiarize themselves with the vocabulary of this book. You are invited to refer to this glossary as you embark on the further exploration of the model and its applications, and to revisit these terms as frequently as needed to strengthen the connection to and comfort with the model.

Beyond grasping these terms cognitively, clinicians are encouraged to use "Parts Language" with children and their families. This in itself is depathologizing and fosters a healing atmosphere centered on acceptance.

Self   The Self is our center, our essence, present from birth. It is who we are and is separate from roles that we play and agendas that we take on. The Self contains powerful qualities such as calmness, curiosity, clarity, compassion, confidence, creativity, courage, and the ability to connect to others. When the internal emotional system is in balance, the Self is in the leadership position, able to bring its qualities to us intrapsychically and interpersonally. These qualities can be experienced in the body and the client is guided to identify the state of Self in session and in their daily life.

Exiles   All of us have experienced trauma, from mild to severe, as the external world does not always provide for our safety and developmental needs. In extreme cases, such as abuse, events have been life threatening. Exiles, especially when experienced in our young and vulnerable years, can threaten to overwhelm our emotional system with sadness, fear, shame, and feelings of inadequacy. We as human beings possess the ability to isolate and prevent these extreme feelings from flooding through and overwhelming us. From their compartmentalized position, Exiles exert a powerful impact on our lives. The ultimate goal of psychotherapy is to gain access to Exiles and to lift the effects of the emotional trauma (burdens) that they carry.

Protective Parts   The intrapsychic system of our personality is organized to protect us and to help us adapt to our family and social environment. When traumatization has been severe, our Protective Parts work very hard to contain Exiles and the emotional burdens they carry. These Parts exist in two general clusters, Managers and Firefighters. While these Parts do buffer emotional pain (Exiles), when they operate in excess they constrain and limit the freedom of Self to be in a leadership position, thereby creating additional difficulties for the intrapsychic and relational systems. Much of therapy is focused on lifting these constraints so that Self can return to its

10

rightful leadership position and so that Exiles can be accessed, unburdened, and healed.

Managers Managers are Protective Parts that are the workhorses of our day-to-day lives. They keep us on track as they keep Exiles out of our conscious experience. Managers focus on keeping us in control of our existence. They are often the people-pleasing, perfectionistic, self-critical, obsessive, and worry Parts of our internal system. In the service of isolating painful Exiles, they inadvertently create problems of their own as they operate on the first-order change level in that they accomplish the blocking of emotional pain but ultimately leave the pain hidden as emotional burdens that limit our flexibility internally and in our relationships. It will be powerfully healing to have clients experience Managers in their bodies and work toward unblending them so that Self energy can be brought to the healing process.

Firefighters Firefighters are activated when painful Exiles break through the barriers protected by Managers. These are quick-fix, reactive, often impulsive Parts that act to extinguish the fiery experience of emotional pain. Firefighters include excessive drinking and drug use, binge eating, promiscuity, cutting, gambling, etc. While these Parts are effective in vanishing pain in the short run, they can have devastating consequences for our physical and emotional health and our relationships with significant others. As with Managers, it will be important to have clients experience Firefighters somatically, appreciate their protective intentions and work toward diminishing their dominance as Self is brought into the leadership position.

Unblending As the good intentions of Protective Parts (Functional Hypothesis) are explored and experienced, it will be possible to unblend them from Self. This results in the client experiencing the healing qualities of Self which can then be applied to the burdens of fear, sadness, shame, and feelings of inadequacy in the healing process. Powerful changes can occur as Self of therapist, child, parents, and siblings are free to interact intrapsychically and interpersonally.

Polarization Protective Parts often interact internally and can become in conflict with one another. People are often pulled from one extreme to another, especially with Managers and Firefighters in competition and conflict. This results in vicious cycles where people feel stuck in a first-order battle such as diet/binge, obsess about homework/avoid homework, compliance/defiance, etc. Successful therapy will operate on a second-order change level, where it will foster Self-leadership to reassure Managers and Firefighters that it is safe to access and bring healing to Exiles.

Part-to-Part Interaction Just as Polarization among Parts occurs on an intrapsychic level, family members can become entangled in Part-to-Part interaction, producing its own vicious cycles. Very often, parents, with good intentions, try to control, manage, and direct their kids. Parents employ coercive measures to get their youngsters to behave, do their homework, and change their habits. This often backfires as these Manager Parts of parents create and trigger painful feelings (Exiles). The child in response will employ his or her own Manager and Firefighter Parts to soothe the Exiles and to counter the assault they feel from parental Parts. The Internal Family Systems MetaModel will work with the child-parent intrapsychic system and relational system to interrupt these unhealthy interactions and foster Self-to-Self interaction. This will be the essence of healing for troubled children and their families.

Self-to-Self Interaction As the constraints of excessive Protective Parts are lifted, Self shines through. Greater freedom for the qualities of Self will enable the child to bring compassion and acceptance to painful Exiles. A parallel process will occur in work with the parents and siblings. As the internal emotional system of each individual becomes balanced, the relational polarizations lighten and the loving qualities of Self are experienced among all family members. Concurrently, as the relational system becomes more balanced with Self-to-Self Interaction dominant, intrapsychic healing is fostered.

Unburdening When there is a sufficient degree of Self energy in the family system, it will feel safe for the emotional pain to be unburdened or lifted from child, siblings, and parents. At times this process can happen spontaneously as the residue of trauma has been worked through in therapy and fear of recurrence is minimized. At other times, the therapist, child, and family can be helped to arrange for an experiential ritual to release emotional pain. The dominance of Self energy will lead to reassurance within each family member that they will be okay and not overwhelmed by life's inevitable disappointments, losses, and other challenges.

2

HISTORICAL ROOTS OF THE INTERNAL FAMILY SYSTEMS THERAPY METAMODEL

Without context, there is no meaning.
Gregory Bateson

The current wave of clinicians can be confidently bolstered by a plethora of research that asserts that psychotherapy as a process of healing is successful. Many investigators have now contributed to an understanding of Common Factors (sometimes called a contextual model, here being defined as the MetaModel) that is a distillation of how psychological struggle and pain can be treated effectively. With much convincing quantitative and qualitative research support, the relative contributions of the Common Factors are differentiated. It appears that client factors account for 40% of improvement in successful outcomes; the therapeutic relationship accounts for 30% of improvement in psychotherapy; placebo, hope, and expectancy account for 15% of the improvement; and specific techniques/models of treatment account for 15% of the improvement Hubble, Duncan, & Miller, 1999). These findings turn the usual discourse about psychotherapy success upside down, as typically clinicians and researchers alike have continued to believe that it is the particular models and specific applications by the therapist that result in therapeutic success.

It would be safe to conclude from this revolutionary finding about psychotherapy that the essence of "what works in therapy" is a curative process present in the client that become activated within a warm and empathic therapeutic relationship. The *artistry* of this process has much to do with the fostering of hope and expectancy and the techniques that draw out the healing aspects in the client. What has emerged is a cutting-edge group of investigators within the psychotherapy integration movement, who are placing their focus on the Self-healing aspects of treatment. These ideas link back to the groundbreaking thinking about Common Factors in psychotherapy put forward by Rosenzweig (1936), Frank and Frank (1991), and Luborsky (1995).

This book resonates with this view of treatment. It is believed that the goodness and resiliency of the human being, the Self, is always present, but often blocked and constrained by Self-protective survival mechanisms. Again, the therapist is seen as the "sculptor" who skillfully brings out the "David" (Self) of the client. The relevance of this view to psychotherapy, as implied by the Common Factors model, is that clients possess their own healing capacity that is brought forth by a therapeutic process that emphasizes listening, empathy, and a drive toward the experience of self-efficacy and Acceptance.

What constitutes the "bringing forth" of these curative processes? How exactly do all ingredients (client, therapist, expectancy, techniques) form together for a recipe of successful therapy? In other words, what are the dynamics and healing processes of the Common Factors? Can the equivalent of Michelangelo's genius be understood and codified for clinicians to employ? Wampold (2010) eloquently parses out the essence of what happens when therapy is successful and traverses all extant models:

> A good working alliance is an indication that the client has accepted the rationale for treatment, the explanation for the treatment, the explanation for the disorder, and is willing to participate in the process of therapy. A critical component of how this leads to change is involved in replacing a maladaptive explanation with an adaptive one. The maladaptive explanation is discouraging because the client cannot see how any action will lead to progress: Put simply, they are stuck. Frank and Frank (1991) would say they are demoralized, whereas Bandura (1997) would say that they have low self-efficacy for change. Acceptance of an alternative explanation changes the client's expectation, which is a critical component of the healing practice. . . . (p. 70)

The contextual model, simply put, places the person and his or her symptoms in various contexts. Explanations about the problems and treatment strategies flow from this contextualization. As Bateson (1972) stated, "Without context, there is no meaning." The potency of one's theory will follow how effectively the therapist has engaged a particular client and that client's cognitive and emotional system in this contextual understanding. Most theories do not emphasize the notion of context but nevertheless are contextualizing. Family Therapy stands out as emphasizing context. In fact, in this model, *the context is the patient.* When a child has a symptom, the family is engaged for both understanding the problem and being tapped into as a resource for change. This does not imply blame of the family. Instead, it views symptoms as adaptational, i.e., each family member is part of an overall choreography as they travel through life. The choreography is survival based.

14

Each model emphasizes a particular context, whether stated overtly or not. If a parent calls saying, "my child cannot pay attention at home and school," depending on which professional gets called, the symptom gets placed in a particular context. The following represents typical options offered in the field of mental health, along with a critique of these options.

The Medical Model will view the symptom in the biological context—a dysfunction of neurotransmitters or a chemical imbalance. The treatment that logically follows would be a trial of medication to correct the disorder within the biological context. The goal is to diminish or eliminate the symptom. When this works successfully, treatment is completed or continues on a maintenance basis. Most often, it is more complicated than this. Often, there is limited success. Sometimes there is no change. Frequently there is some success but worrisome side effects arise. In other words, the context of biology is not simply linear, i.e., there is not a direct hit to erasing the problem but a shake-up to the larger system of body chemistry. This reality often challenges anxious and worried Parts of the child and parents. They can be left feeling thwarted in their efforts, intensifying already elevated feelings of inadequacy. Hopelessness can set in. Similar kinds of results occur when unmanageable kids are placed in residential treatment centers. Their unruliness is contained, but will their exiled feelings of emotional pain be addressed? Will there be family involvement in their treatment? If not, the child will likely return to the same emotional family context following the residential placement. This model places a medical doctor/medication/residential treatment center in the position of external Manager to the child's symptoms/Parts. Short-term gains are likely. Long-term complications are predicted. Biology, traits, and temperament need to be included in the understanding of the child and family. These factors will be explored further as we develop our MetaModel.

Within the psychodynamic model, the clinician would look intrapsychically to understand the child and to intervene. Perhaps the child is struggling with the ability to regulate aggressive impulses or is experiencing anxiety or low self-esteem as a result of feeling different than other students. This contextual view would suggest a strategy of individual play therapy delving into the patient's history, memories, and dreams. The context of child-and-therapist will be an all-important learning laboratory for observing the symptom picture and for making gradual emotively corrective interpretations. Having a safe and secure place to express themselves and just to be, having their Parts accepted and Self encouraged, will provide powerful interventions. Interpretations will have to be supportive, placed in an interpersonal context of Acceptance. There has been a tendency in some analytic circles to force "the truth" upon the patient, to penetrate repressive boundaries. (Wachtel, 2011). Sometimes it seems that the analyst plays a game of "gotcha" with the patient, thinking that it is his or her job to outsmart the patient's defenses with new revelations and insights. When this does not go smoothly, the patient is said to be "resistant." The patient is probably experiencing the therapist as a Manager, and an interpersonal opposition or polarization is likely. When Acceptance is the dominant mode, resistance is viewed as Protective Parts (Managers and Firefighters) of the child that are respected and explored in the treatment within a nurturing setting. The psychoanalytic model, while emphasizing the intrapsychic context along with the therapist-child relationship, typically does not rigorously consider the need for regular treatment of the family context. As we will see throughout this book, without the family systems consideration, there is the likelihood that the child's Protective Parts will need to stay active, sensing that it is not fully safe for Self to be free.

For proponents of learning theory, the symptoms will be viewed as an ineffective reinforcement cycle and poor limit setting by the parents, a teacher or both. This model would place the behavior in context of behavioral antecedents and consequences. Patterson (1982) views child misbehavior as (1) seeking attention by receiving parental aversive responses, i.e., "something is better than nothing" or (2) pushing the parent to give up coercive acts, i.e., "I will escalate my misbehavior so that my parents eventually withdraw and I get my way."

Creating a behavioral chart and employing time-out procedures would be likely interventions within this context. There are many home-based, clinic-based, or school-focused programs that share the components of educating parents regarding more effective patterns of reinforcement of their children's compliant behavior. (Barkley, 1987; Dadds, 1987; Forehand & McMahon, 1981; Horne & Sayger, 1990; Turecki, 1985, Webster-Stratton & Herbert, 1994). Important to note: these programs all promote disengagement of parents from patterns of blame and coercion—in other words, diminishing Manager activity by parents and fostering an Acceptance of the child that they have, traits (warts!) and all, not the idealized child who fills their fantasy. With diminished Manager activity, room is made for the all-important Self-to-Self interaction between parent and child.

Cognitive-behavioral therapists would set their sights on disordered thinking as the context for this behavior. Helping the child to eliminate defeatist Self-statements and replacing them with more statements of self-efficacy would likely be emphasized. For instance, a child with attentional deficits may withdraw or be avoidant of schoolwork, believing that she is a poor student and that the situation is hopeless. In CBT, the therapist would challenge the view of being a poor student and build on strengths for counteracting this belief. Similar work may extend to a parent of this child who believes her child is "damaged" and the future is bleak. Much of therapy filters through cognitive processes, so this approach can be very potent. The worry is that the child (and parent), with the emphasis on "disordered" thoughts, may feel that their feelings are being minimized, dismissed, pathologized, or Managed by the therapist. It will be very important to create an atmosphere of Acceptance so that the negative and painful self-attributions can be processed and healed. Fortunately, the cognitive-behavioral field is evolving to include more of a systems approach both intrapsychically and interpersonally. This "third wave" is centered in Acceptance of emotional pain and making it safe to process powerful and traumatic experiences so that enduring change is possible (Greco & Hayes, 2008; Hayes, Strosahl & Wilson, 1999; Linehan, 1993; Marra, 2005).

Is there a right or wrong model? As has been demonstrated by the Common Factors investigators, the model is presented in a compassionate context to the individual, family, or both. How the model makes sense or not depends on many client factors of receptivity. This is where the artistry of treatment happens. This is what this book is about—the understanding of all contexts that are operative and the skills of a therapist to weave a tapestry that makes sense to the clients in transforming their maladaptive, constrained view into an adaptive and hopeful approach, cognitively, emotionally, and interpersonally.

Before traveling further into the MetaModel and IFS, it will be useful to trace the contributions of thinkers and practitioners in the field of family therapy during the last half century, and to weave these ideas into the understanding of the Functional Hypothesis as a Common Factor in systems thinking and a centerpiece of the process of eliciting the curative aspects of the client. It is this evolving systems approach to understanding and treating emotional struggle that forms the basis for the contextual model of healing. As with most revolutions in thinking, the systems approach represents a paradigm shift (Kuhn, 1962). The essence of this shift is a reversal in treatment philosophy and its applications. Instead of the attempt to eliminate symptoms (medical model, learning model, cognitive behavioral therapy, psychoanalytic applications of repression model) family therapy systems thinking is based on the view of the adaptational/survival view of symptoms. This represents an evolving set of models and therapeutic strategies that invite the symptoms into the treatment room, value and respect their functional purpose, and even harness their energy for transformation and healing.

Bateson (1972, 1979; Bateson, Jackson, Haley & Weakland; 1956/1981) created a paradigm shift in the field of mental health when he and his colleagues in Palo Alto, California, studied families with a schizophrenic member in an anthropological manner, that is, interviewing these families while other team members watched through a one-way mirror. In this groundbreaking work, these participant-observers began to think that bizarre symptoms could be understood when viewed within the family context. In other words, the "disease" of schizophrenia was hypothesized to be an adaptation to skewed and no-escape communication patterns labeled as the "double bind." The symptoms "make sense" when understood in context. Although the Bateson Group's findings have fallen into disfavor amidst the gathering of (still inconclusive) evidence of physiologic factors, and whereas their writings fell prey to the then prevalent thinking (mother-bashing, i.e., shifting blame from patients to mothers), their observations set in motion a new way of viewing psychological symptomatology (Mones, 2003; Mones & Schwartz, 2007). What they said was that symptoms are not pathological aspects of illness. For instance, a highly anxious individual may attempt to control his inner turmoil by imposing (on conscious or unconscious levels) a structure of obsessive thinking. This strategy actually does work to ward off anxiety. However, the solution of obsessive thinking itself becomes a burdensome behavior that constrains the emotional freedom of the patient. The solution then becomes a new problem and likely generates its own new wave of anxiety with new solutions—perhaps now the person begins to soothe himself with excessive drinking that relaxes the pressure of obsessive thoughts but will, over time, deteriorate his health and hamper his relationships. This view mirrors functional models in medicine (Angier, 1991). For instance, physicians began to realize that a physical symptom such as fever is not pathology but the body's defensive strategy to fight infection and kill off bacteria or parasites. However, if unchecked, the fever can create havoc of its own by debilitating the person and compromising survival by creating a weakened state. This is a matter of the solution morphing into a serious problem. In addition, there is a growing set of literature documenting the reactivity of the human immune system to life stress and relationship factors (Scovern, 1999), lending support to a systemic view and functionality of symptoms in medicine.

Bateson's seminal work set in motion the field of family therapy with systems thinking at its core. Essentially, Bateson and colleagues were operating on the path courageously forged by Charles Darwin, the brilliant naturalist and astute observer of survival strategies among animal and human species. Darwin looked at species differentiation as an outgrowth of the drive to survive and asked the basic question: What purpose does this biological feature (beak of finches, etc.) serve in the survival of the individual animal and for the species in general? With that question, Darwin (1859; 1871) revolutionized the field of science and challenged the extant view of life—a view that is still being debated 150 years later (Mayr, 2001).

From Bateson, there is a direct lineage in the models that have evolved in the field of family therapy that embrace the Functional Hypothesis, that is, *psychological symptomatology is context based and linked to emotional adaptation and survival* (Mones & Schwartz, 2007). Therapy that is linked to the Functional Hypothesis would have at its core the need to understand and appreciate the survival nature of the symptom.

18

Instead of defining the symptom as pathology, inherent in the reductionistic medical model approach with its goal of removing the symptom, treatment informed by the Functional Hypothesis would be centered around helping the client to understand and appreciate the protective nature of their symptom and to work systemically (on intrapsychic and interpersonal levels) to make healthier choices that would accomplish the survival need. It is further proposed that this process centers on the essential competence or self-efficacy of the client (Bandura, 1977), a thread that weaves throughout the Common Factors exposition. When the therapist brings out and engages the competence of the client, therapy is on its way to a collaborative journey with successful outcomes.

Prominent family therapists like Murray Bowen and Salvador Minuchin have the Functional Hypothesis indirectly embedded in their models, as traced below. The most direct lineage from Bateson is the Strategic School in the field of family therapy. These practitioners would include Jay Haley, the Mental Research Institute Group, Milan Group, Neurolinguisitc Programming (NLP) and later offshoots, specifically solution-focused therapy, narrative therapy and even postmodernism. The viewpoint presented here will link these models to the centrality of the Functional Hypothesis and to our MetaModel as expressed in the Internal Family Systems Therapy Model.

Bowen (1978) viewed emotional struggle as unresolved anxiety and psychic pain transmitted across and within several generations of a family system. This anxiety is carried by all human beings on an existential level, as our species possesses awareness of the finite nature of living. This inherent anxiety is compounded by emotional trauma and injury experienced in our family of origin. Individuals, couples, and families organize their emotional systems, internal and interpersonal, in ways that attempt to cope with this anxiety. The formation of "emotional triangles" in various combinations (two parents/problem child, marital couple/extramarital affair, couple/alcoholism, etc.) are symptom formations that aim to stabilize and cool down an overheated family climate. Here we can see that triangles serve a survival function in the short run but do not relieve the underlying anxiety and pain that generates this emotional solution in the first place. For Bowen, triangulation is an *interpersonal* strategy of protection for the *intrapsychic* system, resulting in constraints on emotional differentiation and growth of Self. For Bowenian therapists, treatment is aimed at the process of de-triangulation, that is, to remove the emotional detour served by the problem child, extramarital affair, addiction, and so forth, and to have each spouse work on their own Self-differentiation from their respective families of origin. Anxiety around the process of differentiation was the trigger for the construction of the emotional triangle (functional hypothesis/survival strategy) and the liberation of which points the person and family towards health

(Bowen, 1978; Guerin, 1976; Guerin, Fay, Burden & Kautto, 1987; Guerin, Fogarty, Fay & Kautto, 1996; Kerr & Bowen, 1988).

The Structural Family Therapy Model of Minuchin (Minuchin, 1974; Minuchin & Elizur, 1989; Minuchin & Fishman, 1981) posits that symptoms emanate from family typologies that organize around hierarchies, boundaries, and predictable sequences of behavior. On one end of the spectrum are family systems that are characterized by diffuse or unclear boundaries between parental and child generations. In these enmeshed families, there is a heightened emotional reactivity and sensitivity to one another. These families operate with an excess of emotional connection but insufficient allowance for individuation or selfhood. Enmeshed family systems tend to result in symptoms of internalization, that is, anxiety, depression, somatization, and so forth.

On the other end of the spectrum are families that are emotionally disengaged. These families have a dearth of emotional bonding and excessive emotional distance with rigid boundaries between and/or within generations. The most extreme scenario of emotional disengagement represents children who do not form a reliable bond to parental figures, as with children placed in multiple foster care placements over their key developmental years. Adaptation in these families tends to be expressed via symptoms of externalization such as psychopathy, addictions, violence, disregard for the feelings of others, etc.

For Minuchin, symptoms arise from attempts at adaptation (functional hypothesis/survival strategy) in the proximity-distance dimension that are aimed at providing security for the family members. For example, conflict avoidance will "make sense" to a child in an enmeshed family, while defiance may be a key survival strategy for a child from a disengaged family (Mones, 1998a). Interventions are centered on opening up the communication and emotional connection (tightening boundaries/increasing distance) in enmeshed families and fostering emotional connection in disengaged families (opening boundaries/increasing closeness).

Minuchin's thinking resonates with Attachment Theory (Bowlby, 1973), a model that views individuals as operating on a spectrum of secure to insecure emotional connections that will generate strategies of emotional survival. More recently, the Emotionally Focused Therapy Model has employed Attachment Theory as a basis for therapeutic applications (Greenberg & Johnson, 1988; Johnson & Whiffen, 2003; Johnson, 2004). Interventions are geared toward the therapist safely eliciting emotions connected to Attachment Injuries in a marital relationship, often compounded with family of origin trauma. Treatment strategies are aimed at the direct experience, repair, and reassurance from one's spouse so that the Attachment experience is now safe and secure. We will discuss much more on Attachment and repairing Attachment Injury throughout this book.

Strategic Family Therapy began as a direct outgrowth of the Bateson Group's work and has branched into an elaborate tree that reflects the full-blown human creative spirit. At its core, Strategic Family Therapy emphasizes the process of change—how exactly the emotional system of individuals and families becomes constrained (Breunlin, 1999) and how this same emotional system expands its degrees of freedom so as to allow full individuation and differentiation. Strategic Family Therapy is a purist model that views emotional problems as direct attempts at psychological survival. Haley (1980, 1987) coined the phrase "strategic" in describing the process of the therapist formulating treatment strategies to enable families to shift from maladaptive solutions for problems in living to more adaptive strategies. As was the case with his mentor, Milton Erickson (1962; Haley, 1973; Rossi & Ryan, 1992), for Haley symptoms were viewed as metaphors for the family's struggles. In addition, the therapist-client relationship can reflect this struggle, much like transference-countertransference in psychoanalysis. Change the symptom via a system intervention (strategy) that takes into account all reference points of the symptom, and you will alter and maintain new interpersonal relationships that will cope with the presenting issue, as well as new challenges, in a new and healthier manner. Through Haley's work and later with the talented Mental Research Institute (Watzlawick, Weakland, & Fisch, 1974), the Milan Model (Palazolli, Cecchin, Prata, & Boscolo, 1978), and Neurolinguisitic Programming (Bandler & Grinder, 1975) we learn of the powerful nature of symptoms as paradox; we set up strategies and behaviors that serve to protect us from psychological hurt and pain. However, these same strategies, when overemployed, limit our healthy choices. As a Zen Master would do, to change unproductive outcomes of this paradox, the therapist *employs* human nature to improve upon itself. The essence of this approach became labeled as reframing—demonstrating verbally or via behavioral prescription or paradox that symptoms serve a protective purpose but can also create new difficulties. For the strategic therapist, the protective and adaptational nature of symptoms is harnessed for curative purposes.

During the past 30 years, the field of family therapy has extended to even more branching of its evolutionary tree. As our culture has raised its consciousness regarding gender issues, the racial divide, poverty, and cultural diversity, family therapy models have adapted to the spiral of change, even courageously offering critiques of itself (M. Nichols & Schwartz, 2004). As we have included the macro-level of social forces, the concept of adaptation has been amended and the therapeutic circle enlarged. Without sensitivity to these forces, therapists can inadvertently blame the very family systems they have been trying to depathologize.

In response to this new wave of cultural, ethnic, and gender awareness, new models have been offered. The Solution-Focused movement (De Shazer, 1982) proposed that people do not *need* to have problems. Essentially, we

21

possess the strength and resources, and are already exercising these options some of the time. The central theme of solution-focused therapy is that, with the therapist's guidance, clients will discover their reservoir of strengths and reverse from a negative to positive locus. Parallels with cognitive-behavioral therapy are apparent in this model.

Although this model drifts away from and discourages a view of symptoms-as-adaptation, the focus on client competency and resourcefulness is certainly a "bringing forth," a la Michelangelo, of the self-efficacy of the individual.

Postmodern approaches to therapy represent a further branching of the healing tree (Gergen, 2002). Dell (1986) questioned the nature of "paradox" in psychotherapy and connected our field of study to a constructivist creation of meaning. Hare-Mustin and Maracek (1990) and Goldner (1985, 1998) had us take a new look at the construction of gender. Narrative Therapy (Anderson, 1995; White & Epston, 1990) emphasized the collaboration of therapist and family in an equal partnership. Here the therapist elicits the "stories" of her clients, and together they work toward revising their life narrative scripts in a nonjudgmental way. There is considerable focus on externalizing, linking emotional struggles to inequities of society—racism, sexism, emphasis on physical beauty (eating disorders), and so forth. In this approach, blame and shame carried by clients are bypassed as they join with the therapist in a crusade to reform the ills of our culture. Although postmodernists have challenged the notion of the Functional Hypothesis, it may be said that they too are working within this meta-theory—rather than challenging the client to change, their thinking courageously attempts to remove cultural constraints and in so doing liberates the essential competence/self-efficacy (Self) of the client and family members. Roffman (2005) rightly placed functionality in the context of the therapeutic relationship and encouraged the treatment application of the functional hypothesis, but was sure to eliminate the edge of blame in its therapeutic usage, something that Bateson and his original pioneers overlooked—therefore creating a safe, open, fair, and loving emotional climate that the natural goodness and compassion of people will arise to participate in, contribute to, and further generate.

The above review traces the contributions to the contextual model in the family therapy field. It is my view that all models of psychotherapy place the person and his symptoms in various contexts in order to understand and treat them successfully.

In addition to these pioneers of the field of family therapy, the ideas in this book are influenced by many models of psychotherapy integration (Castonguay & Hill, 2007; Gold 2006; Pinsof, 1995; Prochaska & DiClemente, 1984; Stricker, 1994; Stricker & Gold, 2006; and Wachtel, 1977).

3

FAMILY DYNAMICS
The Dance of Adaptation

What Is a Healthy Family?

A healthy family will have parents or caretakers with sufficient levels of Self-energy to be able to raise children in a cooperative partnership as they lead fulfilling lives. The Self-energy available to the parents enables them to provide an atmosphere of attunement and Acceptance, an emotional state that conveys the characteristics of Self to themselves, their partners, their own parents, and their children. In this atmosphere of Acceptance, parents do not try to raise children who conform to the ideal but can accept their child as a unique individual with traits and behaviors that the child owns. Self-led parents raise children in a climate of calmness, curiosity, clarity, compassion, confidence, creativity, and connection. These children in turn grow up to be Self-led and bring their gifts to the world.

Problems of childhood are understood in context—neurobiology, family, school, neighborhood, peer interaction, and ethnic, racial, and cultural influences. In this chapter we will explore the family choreography. As we have seen, childhood symptoms are essentially Protective Parts, buffering the experience of painful Exiles. These Protective Parts activate the Exiles of Parents—powerlessness, sadness, and feelings of inadequacy. In response to the child's behavior, a mother or father will meet the child's Parts (Managers/Firefighters) with their own Protective Parts so as not to become overwhelmed by their own Exiles. This Parts-to-Parts interaction will feed on itself in an unproductive spiral of intensity. The child will stir up the parents' Exiles/vulnerability, and the parents in turn will stir up the child's Exiles/vulnerability in a recursive cycle.

Parents are often relating to their children via Manager Parts—directing them night and day regarding what to wear, what to eat, when to do their homework, etc. Sometimes this is overt, sometimes covert. Children are highly sensitized regarding approval or disapproval from their parents. When children see their parents' approval, they feel good in their bodies; chemicals of pleasure are released (oxytocin, etc.). Their

23

Self is met by parents' Self. When children are met with disapproval, their body feels ill and out of sorts; chemicals of pleasure are blocked and they are in a position of defensiveness. They respond to parents' Manager Parts with their own Protective Manager and/or Firefighter Parts. In this dance we have a Parts-to-Parts scenario. Parts-to-Parts interactions feel unhealthy for parents and children. Sometimes these interactions dominate and there is a toxic climate in the home. The same can arise from Parents being in Firefighter mode. They may be too overwhelmed to step up to parental responsibilities and relate to their children from a depressive or avoidant position. This is frightening for youngsters, and they will need to retreat to a defensive position of protection by activating their own Managers and/or Firefighters. Again we land in Parts-to-Parts territory.

The therapist will need to get to know these Protective Parts of kids and parents. The therapist will need to accept these parts and recognize the positive but overworked intentions of these Parts. The goal, ultimately, is a Self-led child interacting with a Self-led Parent.

Working with kids is different than working with adults. With adults, we are mostly dealing with the residue of emotional trauma. We lift constraints on Self-energy by befriending Manager and Firefighter Protective Parts (Breunlin, 1999). This allows for the healing process of Self-energy brought to Exiles. Therapists know that this emotional journey of healing can be terrifying for the adult client, as the pain of the past is very much alive in the present, but gradually there is a sufficient safety experienced in the knowledge that the danger of emotional injury is past history.

When we work with children, we must remember that they are currently living in a family where trauma is in formation. We are not dealing with the historical remainder of such trauma, but are in the midst and immersed in present family drama and the formation of painful Exiles. Protective Parts can be especially tenacious, as the need for survival is playing out right in front of us! This may limit our access to Exiles as Protective Parts willfully stay in place.

Figure 3.1 depicts the Part-to-Part Interaction of Child and Parent. The author is indebted to Michelle Scheinkman and Mona Dekoven Fishbane (2004) in their formulation of the Vulnerability Cycle that couples struggle with when marital interaction reaches a toxic impasse. Here the chart includes the presence of Self and delineates the complexities of the intrapsychic and relational interaction. Very important contributions from the biological sphere are represented. Of course, it gets much more complicated than this when you add both parents and siblings, all interacting with each other's intrapsychic and relational systems!

Parent-Child Relational System/Part-to-Part Interaction

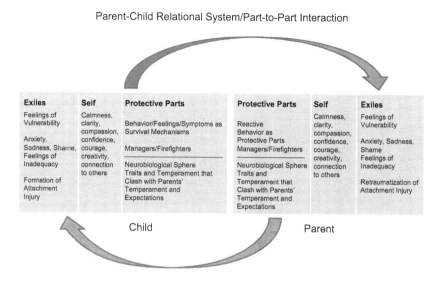

Figure 3.1 Parent-Child Relational System/Part-to-Part Interaction

In the Parts-to-Parts interaction, parents will impose Manager energy or messages to the child in the service of "shaping up" the child's behavior—school performance, habits, behavior, etc. With good intentions, this strategy bypasses the child's Self as it shapes and triggers Exiles of the child, e.g., "my mother is disappointed in me." This results in feelings of sadness and inadequacy and will naturally mobilize the child's Protective Parts, which usually translates into some form of oppositionalism via defiant or even overly compliant behavior. These communications will bypass the parent's Self and instead trigger the parent's Exiles, resulting in his or her feelings of inadequacy, anxiety, and sadness as a parent (person). These Part-to-Part interactions result in vicious cycles that can escalate angrily or lead to withdrawal and resignation, with child and parent feeling misunderstood and invalidated. Similar vicious cycles occur when parents are avoidant of their responsibilities and are unavailable to effectively parent, as their Firefighter Parts are received by the child as disinterested, rejecting, and invalidating as well.

The IFS therapist will work with the child, parents, and family system to foster greater understanding of the survival nature of the Protective Parts (Functional Hypothesis) and to encourage, coach, and model a shift to Self-to-Self interaction as indicated in Figure 3.2.

Transformed Parent-Child Relational System/Self-to-Self Interaction

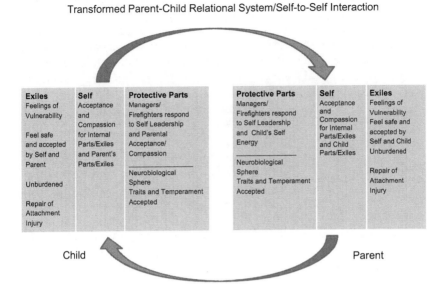

Exiles	Self	Protective Parts		Protective Parts	Self	Exiles
Feelings of Vulnerability	Acceptance and Compassion for Internal Parts/Exiles and Parent's Parts/Exiles	Managers/ Firefighters respond to Self Leadership and Parental Acceptance/ Compassion		Managers/ Firefighters respond to Self Leadership and Child's Self Energy	Acceptance and Compassion for Internal Parts/Exiles and Child Parts/Exiles	Feelings of Vulnerability
Feel safe and accepted by Self and Parent						Feel safe and accepted by Self and Child
						Unburdened
Unburdened		Neurobiological Sphere		Neurobiological Sphere		
		Traits and Temperament Accepted		Traits and Temperament Accepted		Repair of Attachment Injury
Repair of Attachment Injury						

Child   Parent

Figure 3.2 Transformed Parent-Child Relational System/Self-to-Self Interaction

Here there is Acceptance of the child's vulnerabilities and a letting go of an "agenda" for shaping the child into the expectations or fantasies of the parent. The parent listens more than she manages.

The parent is open-minded and open hearted and can better attend to his or her own Exiles of fear, sadness, shame, and inadequacy. Opening of the emotional system allows the child to breathe more freely and allows for greater safety to be his own Self within his family system. Both parent and child are on their way to a more loving and healthy interaction.

Family Context, Rules, Neurobiology of Attachment, and Individuation

In this chapter I will summarize useful concepts and processes to apply greater understanding to children and their families. The concepts have been contributed from Psychodynamic Theory, Bowen Theory, Structural Family Therapy, Strategic Models of Systems Therapy, Cognitive Behavioral Therapy, Dialectical Behavior Sensorimotor Therapy, Acceptance and Commitment Therapy, Emotionally-Focused Therapy, and Attachment Theory of Child Development. All of these significant contributions will be interwoven with Internal Family Systems Therapy vocabulary and applications.

From the beginning, my preference as a clinician was to specialize in the treatment of children. The dominant model of the time was to treat children individually in play therapy while another therapist worked with the mother (and hardly ever involved the father!).

Child patients responded to the quiet Acceptance of their sessions and were soothed by the nurturing nature of open-ended play and projective expression. The therapy room became a place where the child felt depathologized as Self-energy was celebrated. The child felt good about himself and could gain a sense of self-efficacy and confidence. Often, these healing processes were thwarted, as only minimal generalization occurred at home and school. While some parents learned to parent in a Self-led manner, most continued to feel confused and frustrated by behavior at home as well as negative reports from teachers.

As the field of Family Therapy was developing, I dabbled. I began to include parents in my treatment and quickly expanded sessions to include parents, the identified child patient, and siblings. Therapy was much more complicated and much more rewarding. I now was seeing before my own eyes the child's symptoms in context—the child's behavior now made sense when viewed within the family choreography. I was intrigued and now was able to expand upon the individual work of healing children and view the family itself as my patient. The work deepened. The results were more durable. Here is what I learned as I studied family systems and worked with families, first in community mental health centers and then in private practice:

The whole is greater than the sum of its parts. The family itself is an organism, not just a group of individuals. The family operates with its own dynamics of group preservation. The family is in constant developmental flux as two adults are launched from their respective families of origin, meet one another, fall in love, marry, and develop their careers. They have children and become parents with awesome responsibility.

Children grow from small to big with significant developmental milestones that reflect gains and losses on behavioral and emotional planes. As all of this is happening, many other gains and losses occur within and beyond the nuclear family, including economic pressures, marital cohesion and tensions, sibling conflict, gains and losses for each parent's family of origin, health concerns for significant family members, the dissolution of many marriages, and deaths of significant relatives. In addition, the world continues to spin and societal forces of gender, race, and, for some, the turbulence of natural disasters and civil wars affect the family unit. The family as a whole will need to navigate this daunting array of developmental issues. At all stages the family organism will try to achieve equilibrium and homeostasis. When emotional struggle ensues and clear resolution falters, Protective Parts will enter to help each family member cope. Attachment will vary from secure to insecure. Parents and children, consciously and unconsciously, will be putting their feet on the brake or accelerator as they round the sharp curves of the life cycle.

Sometimes the ride will be smooth; sometimes quite bumpy. Each family will have its story. The therapist needs to listen carefully to this story. The "diagnosis" of the "problem" child will be a contextual formulation of the child in this story. The formulation will be the Functional Hypothesis as described in the previous chapter. The child's symptoms will be viewed as an attempt at surviving within this family story.

Families metacommunicate: Beginning with the groundbreaking work of Gregory Bateson and colleagues in the 1950s, when viewing family interaction it was observed that parents and their children are able to communicate on two planes, sometimes simultaneously. For example, a parent can express loving words on a verbal/cognitive plane (Self-expression) while communicating cold and rejecting feelings on a non-verbal/emotional level (Parts activated). Children try to make sense out of this. They usually attend most powerfully to nonverbal communication, and Protective Parts take shape in order to protect against the hurt and pain from seeing disappointment mirrored back to them from those who are most important and possess the most power in their lives. When their natural Self-energy is met by the Self-energy of parents, it will feel safe to bring this energy into the internal and interpersonal world. However, when their natural Self-energy is met with responses from Parts of parents' internal emotional system, the child's Parts will enter as protection in the experience of an imperfect, insecure Attachment experience. Mind and body will adjust to "make sense" of incongruities of experience.

The Parts will gain prominence as protection against this disappointment and disillusionment. The degrees of freedom for Self-expression begin to diminish, directly proportional to the degree of negativity in the eyes of their caretakers. The Self is constrained and the child will operate in the world via Parts that protect.

The non-escape clause: In families, there is an existential truth that children have awareness of, consciously and/or unconsciously. They are "stuck" with their family of origin, always. You will always be the son or daughter to these particular parents; the brother or sister to these particular siblings. Children can grow up and not call home or move to another continent, but this existential truth applies to all. In order to cope with this psychological fact, children develop strategies of survival. These strategies are in the spatial dimension and time dimension. In the spatial dimension, children learn that they can control how close and how far they will allow themselves and other family members to be from one another. As you observe oppositionalism, you will see how children can push away (angry interaction) and draw close (parents' Management) while at the same time offering buffering from uncomfortable Exiled feelings. Oppositional Parts evolve and work effectively for emotional survival within the family but constrain Self-energy. Being withdrawn or depressed is another strategy in this dimension, as children can soothe themselves and remain on a safe "island" within the family. Depressed Parts are protective but, as with oppositional Parts, constrain Self-leadership.

Alternatively, children can also navigate via the time dimension. Young children can act as little parents in a pseudo-mature show of behavior. Older children can remain very childlike and struggle with taking responsibility and maturity, sometimes unable to launch into adulthood. These are examples of the types of Parts that help children survive the non-escape reality of their lives. They will depend on these Parts, which at times become so blended with Self that others will assume that this is the essence of the child, e.g., "Susie is a depressed child." Therapy will aim to un-blend the Protective Parts from Self so that the child can operate freely and fluidly, intrapsychically and interpersonally.

Homeostasis: Families are constantly in flux. At one point in time, children are growing physically and cognitively in the contexts of home, school, and peer group, parents are managing the home, their relationship with their children, with each other, their jobs, peer relations, their health, their relationships with their respective families of origin, and the melding of two family systems. Issues of economic and cultural status are always at play, contributing to a sense of place on a continuum of powerless to powerful. The family life cycle is constantly changing (Carter & McGoldrick, 1989; Mikesell, Lusterman & McDaniel, 1995). In order to provide safety and security, parents, children, extended family, and significant others make choices to try to keep the engine running smoothly. If there is excess change, this creates anxiety in the family system, with parents and children adjusting and adapting on intrapsychic and relational planes. In essence, the family system is attempting to maintain equilibrium and homeostasis. This is done on conscious and unconscious levels, navigating through times of gain and loss for each family. The therapist, in encountering a child and family system, will make note of how well the family is doing in this process of adaptation and especially what the trade-offs are to the choices made in the service of providing protection and safety.

Attachment and neurobiology: Human beings are social animals. Along with needs for food, clothing, and shelter, they need and seek relationships as dependent children and throughout the life cycle. The seeking of relationships corresponds to our need for physical and emotional security. In the family of origin we learn how reliably we can trust getting close to other human beings. There is no perfect parenting. At some points along the developmental pathway parents will disappoint, be too preoccupied, or not be there when the child needs them to be. Sometimes parents will puncture acceptable boundaries and assault their children, as in extreme verbal abuse, physical abuse, and sexual assault (Mones & Panitz, 1994).

All children will have less-than-perfect Attachment histories. All children will have Attachment Injuries from mild to severe. Just as the auto-immune system protects us (imperfectly) from germs and disease, our emotional system will offer protection from these injuries and punctures of Attachment. Many of our Protective Parts will buffer the pain of these injuries and serve as walls that attempt to disallow devastation from future emotional assaults. While these walls keep us vigilant against further disappointments, they also keep us away from the experience of satisfying human connection. Protection against further hurt comes at a cost and disallows the connection that provides for physical and emotional security. Therapists regularly encounter Protective Parts that are solutions, but these solutions often morph into new and serious problems.

Bowlby (1973) was the pioneer in the field of Attachment, focusing his lens on the varied styles of infant-maternal emotional connection. Bowlby's observations led to a categorization of Attachment styles from secure to insecure. For several decades this area of study remained in the academic/research/child development realm. In the past several years, clinicians have brought the process of Attachment into the study of human relationships throughout the life cycle and into our diagnostic schema for understanding and treating our clients, particularly for very challenging cases. At this point, it is useful to think of cases that were previously viewed as "resistant." A nonpathologizing view is that these clients experience change as extremely difficult and even as a threat to their survival. With such clients, progress in treatment leads to a massive wave of anxiety as they experience success and growth despite potentiating loss, rejection, and abandonment from key figures in their lives (Masterson, 1976). This powerful and perplexing scenario is often experienced directly in the client-therapist relationship. This can now be viewed not as resistance but as a clinging to strategies of emotional survival while struggling with an Attachment Injury. These clients reflexively have Parts that undermine forward movement.

My most dramatic experiences of this dynamic have been in working with kids in multiple foster care placements. Rosario, age 14, was referred for aggressive behavior In and out of school. He had been in five different foster homes since infancy. His "expectation" was to be uprooted to another family and school. Rosario viewed the external world as unreliable and threatening. His internal emotional system was largely organized to defend internally and interpersonally with lack of constancy and dependable Attachment. In therapy, I met his Parts: one was extremely eager to please, one was hypervigilant to signs of disapproval, one was frequently testing the limits on behavior, being "bad" so that adults would be challenged in their ability to remain accepting and approving. This last Part was tenacious as it served as a Protector of Abandonment—Rosario would "mess up" his behavior (Firefighter), thereby garnering some control (Manager) of his being terrified of the impending abandonment. In other words, Rosario actively rejected others before they had a chance to reject him. I invited in all these Parts (along the way needing much calming of my own Manager Parts and, frankly, scared Parts as he played out very aggressive maneuvers in challenging me in the therapy room). I kept my eye on the prize—his Exiles of sadness and feelings of abandonment, and I did my best to be a steady, reliable figure to him. I did considerable work with the foster parents, school, and social service agency, advocating for special educational placements and therapeutic support during his school day. There were many ups and downs. I viewed this as "predictable unpredictability" and had Rosario learn about all of his Parts and struggles. Over a long span of time, and Rosario being fortunate to have foster parents who stayed the course during the balance of his adolescence, Rosario's volatility calmed. He was able to form friendships, graduate high school, and stay steady enough to enroll in training and then work in the field of auto mechanics. He was able to enter the adult world and take on its responsibilities and challenges.

In recent years, the field of Attachment and human emotional relatedness has expanded into the field of neurobiology (Siegel, 1999; Fishbane, 2008, van der Kolk, 1987, 2006 ; Ogden, Minton & Pain, 2006). Emotional reactivity can be viewed as a current precipitant—for example, a child refusing to do his homework, linking into an emotional store of memory for the child (child feeling bad and being criticized for his deficits) and the parents (parents feeling powerless or inadequate in their family of origin and (prior to a complex web) experiencing disappointment due to their idealized image of their child) as a complex web of neuronal/hormonal bodily reactions. It is now known that the past storage of painful feelings exists in the amygdala, part of the limbic/emotional system of the brain. This is enormously useful for our survival, as this memory store keeps us vigilant and adaptive, ready for future disappointments. This memory store, akin to Tolle's (2005) "Pain Body," is very powerful and generates what for our IFS MetaModel would be our Protective Parts. Our Managers and Firefighters react to perceived threats by activating the approach/avoidance (fight-or-flight) adaptive behaviors and strategies (Selye, 1956). The sympathetic nervous system appears to be the location for the fight-or-flight mobilization under threat or perceived threat, the latter being often what therapists encounter in the therapy room. The parasympathetic nervous system immobilizes our bodies under extreme threat. Porges (2011), in his polyvagal theory, describes a very basic evolutionary adaptation linked to the parasympathetic immobilization. When individuals cannot utilize fight or flight and when immobilization is life threatening, as in rape or abuse by parents or other authority figures, they can remove themselves from the situation while staying alive by fainting or dissociating. They have survived, but at quite a cost, as their relational world is constantly in a state of danger and alert. This neurobiological research appears to parallel astute clinical observations of the dissociative process described by Schwartz & Goulding (1995) and Bromberg (2006).

The amygdala/emotional brain is counterbalanced by the prefrontal cortex, viewed as the rational, "chief executive officer" in our brains, helping us to make choices and decisions from a logical point of view. Some of us appear to have a dominant limbic system and are highly emotive, with little filtering by logic and reasoning (often these clients are diagnosed as "borderline"). Others of us have a dominant prefrontal cortex, where thinking logically is the order of the day, and, when working in the extreme, where little emotion is entering into experience (often these clients are diagnosed as "obsessional"). Ogden and colleagues (2006) view the range of behavioral choices in many clients as either "hyperaroused" (clients dominated by emotion, action, and impulse [controlled by the amygdala in the lower brain]) to clients who are "hypoaroused" (clients dominated by logic, caution, and inhibition [controlled by the prefrontal cortex upper brain]). These investigators posit a "window of tolerance" that allows for a balance of emotion and reasoning, and have developed sensorimotor therapy to work with top-down (cultivating emotional experience in the face of logic dominance) or bottom-up (cultivating logical, executive functioning in the face of emotion dominance) cases.

In relationships, each person's neurobiological system interacts with another's neurobiological system—parent-child, spouse-to-spouse, sibling-to-sibling, along with each individual's amygdala–prefrontal cortex dance—and I believe a family's emotional system and neurobiology is greater than the sum of its parts. It is posited that "mirror neurons" exist as family members interact behaviorally and influence the synaptic network for each individual in the relationship (van der Kolk, 1987, 2006). The therapist is faced with all of this and is challenged to observe, organize, and intervene so that intrapsychic and relational healing can occur. In neurobiological terms, the therapist will be "re-programming" the complex neuronal circuits described, and I think, only estimated here (Fishbane, 2008).

Individuation

Human nature is such that children grow from small to big, physically, cognitively, and emotionally. They are programmed for this. Their "job," or default position, is to grow and blossom into the fullness of their "flower." As is the case for flowers, the environmental conditions are not always ideal—water supplies may be limited, sun may be too scarce or too severe, stormy behavior may interrupt the growth process or uproot the plant altogether.

This default position for kids is to individuate, to grow into the full fruition of their Selfhood. In one way or another, conditions for full growth may be compromised—parents may be limited due to physical illness and/or emotional constraints on qualities of Self needed to guide the child safely and securely. Under such constraints, youngsters will call upon their Protective Parts as survival mechanisms and may overly rely on these Parts to keep them on their individuative path.

The clinician, in assessing the child and family, needs to formulate a good sense of how open or closed is the path to individuation, also referred to as Differentiation (Bowen, 1978). When encountering a family, it will be important to evaluate this dimension. Does the child's growth and success have a clear path, supported by parents, siblings, and extended family? To what extent is a child's growth met with a loving gaze and encouragement or, because of constraints of Self mentioned above, to what extent does a child's behavior trigger anxiety, sadness, or both in the internal emotional system of the parents and other key figures? How far is the child allowed to go from the root system of their family of origin? The therapist needs to watch and listen closely to this aspect of the family context, as therapy represents change and support of individuation for child, siblings, and parents (and extended family). This energy, sought out by the family and opposed simultaneously, will likely encounter the Protective Parts of family members that experience growth as a threat to the emotional survival of the family emotional system (Masterson, 1976). The therapist will need to view these forces not as pathology but as adaptive and survival based. Treatment will need to address this very important and very powerful force over and over again.

The reader will notice that the process of individuation is linked to all the dimensions listed above—family as greater than the sum of its parts, meta-communication, the non-escape clause and, most powerfully, Attachment.

Part Two

THERAPEUTIC APPLICATIONS OF THE INTERNAL FAMILY SYSTEMS METAMODEL
Doing Child-Focused Family Therapy

In this section of the book, the theory and MetaModel put forward in Part One will be applied to the nuts and bolts of doing child-focused family therapy. The ideas conveyed here flow directly from the MetaModel. Chapter 4 will cover, in detail, the clinical assessment of children and their families in a step-by-step sequence, including the rationale for this process. Chapter 5 describes the organizing concepts and principles for child and family treatment, with emphasis on the Functional Hypothesis and Acceptance as the Common Factors of the healing process.

Chapter 6 covers treatment of the intrapsychic emotional system of kids, with an emphasis on working on their Protective Parts—Managers and Firefighters. Use of play therapy with specific techniques and games are included. In Chapter 7, the all-important process of healing Attachment Injuries of children is emphasized and understood as where the focus needs to be with our most challenging cases. Including siblings in treatment as key members of the family and emotional environment of the identified child client, as well as the importance of the psychology of sibling influence, is explored in Chapter 9. Special consideration of the struggles of teens, along with specific strategies for their treatment, is explicated in Chapter 10. Delving back inside the child's emotional experience as manifested in the body via somatic expression is the topic of Chapter 11, with special thoughts on how the struggles of youngsters become manifested via somatic communication, alongside suggestions for how the therapist can gain access to this realm of experience. Throughout Part Two are special considerations for therapy with families of separation, divorce, single parenthood, and remarriage.

4

CLINICAL ASSESSMENT
OF CHILDREN AND THEIR
FAMILIES

This section represents an *integration* of Structural Therapy, Bowen Theory, Strategic Therapy, and Sensorimotor Therapy, all woven into our Internal Family Systems MetaModel. This approach to treatment has been found to be successful with a wide range of child problems. Contributions from each model are noted in brackets.

How Does the Family Therapist Effectively Assess a Child-Focused Problem?

While there are a plethora of models describing how to understand child symptomatology, the approach presented here is integrative in nature and is a distillation of more than three decades of clinical work with children and their families. Techniques and strategies are accompanied by a running conceptual commentary. It is recommended to use this structure with children from preschool through adolescence. The reader is encouraged to incorporate concepts and methods in keeping with his or her approach to this work.

Is It Important to Separate a Phase of Assessment from the Subsequent Treatment?

When a parent (still, most typically, a mother) calls a therapist for help with their youngster, a complex process is set in motion. The referral may come directly from the parent, and the encouragement for treatment has likely also come from a teacher, social services agency, or court. Often the parent is bewildered and is feeling hopeless regarding her own inability to help her child. Child symptoms are usually derivative of a multitude of processes, including neurobiology, temperament, family history, current stress, economic status, and larger cultural issues related to ethnicity and gender. This presents a major challenge to even the very experienced therapist.

When the family therapy field was in its infancy, the recommended starting point was to begin treatment immediately with a session that included parents and children. While this session afforded the therapist a chance to view the family at its most vulnerable, and perhaps when it was most receptive to help, this also was a highly anxiety-ridden beginning for treatment. It was not uncommon for a parent (again, most typically, the mother) to be dragging in a spouse who wanted nothing to do with the process, an adolescent who immediately shut down in the session by pulling his hat over his eyes while slouching on the therapist's couch, along with a hyperactive younger child literally spinning around the treatment room, opening and closing drawers and closet doors and plopping down occasionally on a parent's lap, asking to go to the bathroom. Needless to say, this is a daunting scene for the therapist, who is trying to engage with the family, get some beginning understanding of the content and history of the presenting problem, and also set fees and arrange for the scheduling of sessions. The family, given this chaos, would likely escalate their anxiety and often feel shame at their exposure and impotence. This is not a good way to begin.

It is much more effective to slow down the process by separating a period of assessment from the actual treatment. Stating this to a parent on the telephone can be a great relief to them. It gives them some time to tell their story without the pressure to begin a process that they barely understand. Likewise, structuring an assessment phase gives the therapist needed timing and pacing to try to figure out how to help the family.

Parents by and large do not know about family therapy. Even if they have heard of this approach to treatment, they probably do not think about their child's problem from a systems perspective. Most likely they hope to bring their child to an expert who will "fix" the child, much like a pediatrician or dentist would treat their child for some medical problem. They will likely picture a scene that includes the child patient talking to a therapist while the parent waits passively in the waiting room. This approach to treatment does not represent pathology or resistance; it is the typical way a parent thinks and feels about seeking a solution to their child's difficulties. Much work needs to be done in order to inoculate the family to view the presenting problem from a systems perspective and to participate in the healing process.

It is, therefore, very useful to spend time on the telephone describing the need for an assessment phase that precedes the actual treatment and spelling out the sequence of sessions that will comprise this process.

The Initial Telephone Call

When a parent makes the initial call, it is important and *therapeutic* for the therapist to speak directly to her (ideally, to both parents if possible). If there is a structure in a clinic or agency whereby a secretary screens the case and handles administrative matters, it is still important for the therapist to make direct contact by phone with the parent(s) prior to the first face-to-face session.

When a parent calls, the therapist should provide approximately 20 minutes of time to listen to the parent's concerns and to orient the parent to the structure of the assessment process. It takes a lot for a parent to call—typically, many strategies to solve the problem have been tried at home; there likely have been conferences with the school regarding the youngster's academic and/or behavioral struggles; friends and extended family may have chimed in with suggestions. It is likely that the parent has consulted with a previous therapist or two. Parents are likely confused at the array of choices in the mental health field: will medication be the solution, and what exactly is child therapy? Parents may have heard about psychoanalytic approaches, cognitive-behavioral approaches in addition to family therapy. How could they possibly sort out these choices? Most likely they have called because a trusted teacher, school psychologist or social worker, or relative or friend has recommended this therapist. A key factor always is economic—they've called because the therapist is on the "provider list" of their insurance plan. Parents are typically feeling a combination of helplessness and shame regarding their child's difficulties. It takes an act of courage and strength to pick up the phone and make this call. All this and more the therapist needs to be aware of.

First and foremost, the initial phone call is the start of the engagement process of the therapist and family. So, providing time, listening carefully, and respecting the concern and anxiety about this process all need to be conveyed. Entrusting one's child and family to the care of this professional is a big step that needs to be appreciated.

The therapist begins by asking the parents to describe the concerns that they are seeking help with. The therapist can ask some clarifying questions and should offer a sense of understanding of what is being communicated. Most of all, the therapist should convey an optimistic attitude regarding the nature of help.

After listening a bit to the parents, the therapist takes some time to describe the way he or she typically approaches a child-focused case. Mentioning assessment as a start is helpful and a relief to the parent. The therapist then proceeds to describe a five-session assessment process:

Session One will be a meeting with *both parents* in order to hear more about their concerns and to team up with them in order to help their child. It is not uncommon for a mother to state that it will be very difficult for her husband to attend a session because of his long work hours, business travel schedule, etc. Or the mother may state that the husband "really doesn't believe in therapy" or, "he relies on me to handle things that come up with the kids." These comments are based on basic beliefs inherent to this particular family within our current society. This is a critical point in the establishment of a systems approach to treatment. The therapist needs to be very firm about needing both parents to attend the first session, as both are important in the child's life, and that the child will need to see both working together to solve the presenting problems. The therapist will emphasize the "team effort approach" of building on family strengths, not blaming parents. (It will be noted that this approach is linked to the Solution-Focused model of building on strengths, not focusing on problems, in order to help families.) Should the mother emphasize that her husband will be away on a business trip or could only attend an evening appointment, the therapist needs to be very flexible—I'd recommend waiting until the business trip is completed and making time that is convenient for the family to whatever extent possible. Also, offering to speak directly to the father can be very helpful in many cases. On the phone, highlighting the importance that he plays in the youngster's life is usually effective in convincing him to attend the first meeting. The importance of this structure, both parents involved in child-focused family therapy, cannot be emphasized enough. This will immediately establish the parents as the executive system in the family. While it may shake up the homeostasis a bit, it will ultimately be an important curative factor for the family system. (The reader will note the use of executive system of the parents as a crucial concept from the Structural Family Therapy Model pioneered by Salvador Minuchin, MD.)

Following the discussion regarding the importance of beginning with the parents' session, the therapist should briefly describe the subsequent sequence of sessions as follows: The second session will be for the identified child patient only. The third session will be for the identified child patient as well. The fourth session is for the entire nuclear family. The fifth session will be a feedback session for the parents in which the therapist will present his or her impressions and collaboratively plan a treatment strategy for the child and family. The notion of an assessment phase to precede the treatment is usually received very well by the parents. Each family is unique and each set of problems is a special puzzle to decipher and treat. It is difficult to prescribe exactly how to conduct the assessment. There are, however, key elements of this process to be accomplished by the family therapist. A session-by-session description of the important elements of the assessment process, along with rationale, follows. (Please note that the examples given employ the terms "husband" and "wife" for the purposes of organizing the discourse for the reader. The assessment process and all that follows are fully applicable and have been equally successful in work with committed partners who are not married as well as same-sex couples raising a family.)

Session One: Initial Parents Session

As mentioned above, the inclusion of both parents is a crucial structure for a systems approach to treatment. I have found that while a father may be initially grumpy with regard to the investment of time and money in this process, he is most often pleased to be included as an important player in the life of his youngster. Most often, fathers rise to the occasion. While on the surface it appears that they are happy to be work focused while their wives handle the endless responsibilities of child care and home management, it is often the case that men feel lonely and emotionally isolated and yearn to be more connected in a meaningful way to family life. Additionally important is the impact on the children, especially the identified child patient, to see both parents involved in handling a problem situation. Often, the identified child patient has been part of emotional triangulation (Bowen Theory), i.e., his symptoms provided a deflection of anxiety and conflict in the parental sphere. Seeing that both parents are together meeting with the therapist can be a great relief, as now the therapist can move into the triangle and the child can potentially be relieved of this burdensome family role.

The most important task of the initial session with the parents is engagement. The therapist needs to appreciate the time, effort, and courage expended by the parents in seeking help. Asking the parents about their feelings in regard to coming to the session is useful. A helpful way to begin is to ask about strengths and successful aspects of their family (Solution-Focused approach). This can relax the parents a bit, diminish the shame factor, and give them an experience of stating and sharing some pride in their family. The therapist should take note of these positive family attributes as a foundation to build on. It is also helpful to observe how the parents interact when not focused on problems.

Next, the parents are asked to describe the difficulties currently occurring in the family. It is important to note whether they are sympathetic to their child's issues or whether they have reached a point of toxicity, that is, anger and powerlessness regarding being able to help their child. The therapist will also note the sameness and differences in how the parents describe the child. Are they together in their approach or is there much dissension?

After an initial overview of the problem description, the therapist gently leads the parents to consider certain questions. The purpose of these questions is on one level to gather important information and on another level to begin to inoculate the parents to thinking about their child and family via a systems framework and belief system. In the therapist's mind is the map that will guide him or her throughout the assessment and treatment—placing the presenting problem in a multifaceted context in order to understand the problem from a systems perspective and, given this understanding, being able to formulate a Functional Hypothesis from which will flow treatment strategies. The Functional Hypothesis will be presented as the culmination of the assessment process in the parent feedback session.

The therapist will ask about the various contexts in which the presenting problem is embedded. It is enormously helpful to construct a genogram of the entire family system to include at least three generations (Bowen Theory). The genogram provides a pictorial summary of the family system (McGoldrick, 2008). Some therapists will sketch the genogram while doing the interview. Others will do so after the session, which is my own preference. I prefer to not be encumbered by pads and pencil while I am interacting and observing the clients. This choice is purely up to the style of the therapist. It should also be noted that the construction of the genogram is not a one-shot deal and should reflect an evolving process throughout the assessment and, indeed, throughout the treatment.

The therapist will ask about when and where the symptoms occur: home (more so when mom or dad or siblings are present?) or school (under what circumstances, e.g., structured activities or unstructured, certain teachers, with particular students, etc.). Questions about significant others (siblings, grandparents, aunts, uncles, housekeepers, etc.) are very important. Questions about significant family events may be relevant (losses of key family members, illnesses, job loss or stress, economic difficulties, etc.).

If it does not come out naturally in the conversation, it will be important to trace the biological nature of the child. Is the child of average height or weight, or larger or smaller than average? Is the child on the passive side or active side, or perhaps "hyper"? Does the child struggle with any particular aspects of academic subjects? Is the child's temperament outgoing or reserved in social situations? Does the child have any bodily sensitivities or allergies? Are there any medical concerns that were encountered and continue to be treated and monitored? How does the child relate to doctor's visits? How does the child tolerate physical pain?

An important question to ask the parents is about their reaction to the difficulties. This allows the therapist to begin to connect with the parents' emotional systems (Internal Family Systems MetaModel). For full healing to occur, it will be crucial for the therapist to tune into the internal emotions of the parents, and to eventually unburden them of issues based on their own life conflicts and traumas that are linked to their child's problems. As previously emphasized, the child's issues can be understood when placed in multiple contexts. *There is a relationship that parents (and child) have to the symptoms*. Exploring very closely how they feel toward the problem is a crucial question. The goal is to identify and differentiate Parts that are critical and/or attempting to ameliorate the symptoms—the Managers and Firefighters. Creating room (internally) for Self-energy to bring empathy and curiosity to the symptoms is a key process of healing.

Before concluding the session, the parents should be asked for some feedback on their experience with the therapist. The subsequent sessions in the assessment phase should be described again (a mother may not remember details of the telephone conversation; a father may not have been told much about this).

Parents can be coached as to what to say in preparing their youngster for therapy. As usual, parents will vary in their style. Some parents obsess about this process, worried and sensitive to their child's reactions. Other parents will avoid telling their child until the last minute, perhaps an hour or two prior to the session. The therapist can offer some suggestions for this process. It should be noted, however, that any giving of "advice" will be received by the parents in a multitude of ways. The most likely is for them to glaze over and ultimately do it their own way. This is a normal reaction and a key aspect of therapy and will be treated in a separate section. The therapist should encourage the parents to emphasize to the child the positive potential of "improving family relations" and the likelihood of participation by the whole family. De-emphasize the focus on the child. De-emphasize an attitude of blame towards the child, if at all possible. Give the child at least two to three days notice so that he can be mentally ready for this new and stressful event that is being imposed on him by the parents. Above all else, be respectful and acknowledge the child's feelings about beginning a therapy process.

One simple intervention that can be recommended is for the parents to observe and even keep a log of when, where, and in whose presence the problem occurs over the next few weeks. This is very often a key intervention in behavioral models. Here, the potency of this recommendation is to have the Selves of the parents create some space by unblending from the child's problems. It begins the process of untangling a Part-to-Parts interaction and moving toward a Self-to-Self interaction by moving the parents back a bit. Their emotional reactivity can be lessened and so that they can join together as "personal scientists" (Mahoney, 2003), or neutral observers, joining in the venture with the therapist to understand and help their youngster. The assessment sessions are cultivating a team approach.

Session Two: Identified Child Patient

The second session of the assessment process is for the identified child patient and therapist. Some family therapists will ask, why isolate the child from the family at this early point in the evaluation? Aren't you giving the message that the child's problems are separate from the larger family system? These are good questions and, indeed, this strategy is a controversial one.

The reason I have found an individual session to be a wise choice is that the parents expect that the therapist, a child psychology expert, will get to know their child and formulate some opinions about his difficulties. As mentioned above, the parents look to the therapist much as they would a consultation with a pediatrician. It is important for the therapist to join with this expectation of being in the "expert role," as this will build confidence and credibility with the parents. It would be unwise to try to dissuade the parents from this expectation, as it will likely leave them feeling unsure that the therapist has a good sense of their child. In psychometric literature, this concept is called "face validity," i.e., a test that is constructed to measure intelligence, spatial ability, etc., should seem to the test taker to be relevant to the subject matter. For the parents, a therapist who will help their child and family should meet and evaluate the identified child patient.

Another reason to meet individually with the identified child patient is that this youngster is probably hurting emotionally and feeling very vulnerable. This would be the case even (or especially) for the child whose behavior, on the surface, appears bold and defiant. If the first meeting for such a youngster were to be in the presence of his parents, who would likely point out his shortcomings (activated blaming Parts) and flaws, this would leave the child feeling ever more vulnerable (activated Exiles) and would likely "shut down" (activated Protective Parts) early in the treatment process. By meeting with the therapist one-on-one, the youngster is given an opportunity to express his feelings openly regarding participation in this process and to have a chance to engage with the therapist without competing against the parents' viewpoints, as is the case at home. The child's Self will likely feel much less threatened when being greeted by the Self of the therapist.

In addition, identified child patients are in a formidable role in most families. As mentioned above, they are typically a key player in emotional triangles (Bowen Theory) in the family system. This is both an overly powerful and very frightening position for a young person. The therapist will be viewed, even by the most oppositional youngster, as a potential substitute in entering the parental-conflict triangle, and the child would welcome a respite from this unhealthy position. At the same time, the therapist represents change, an assault on homeostasis leading the child to be wary of this process. This child is in inner turmoil and seeks healing. By engaging with her, the therapist makes it clear that therapy is aimed at helping with this internal emotional strife and disequilibrium (Internal Family Systems MetaModel). An alliance with the therapist establishes hope for change. It is, after all, hope for changing the system (at times while trying to hold the system together) that is embodied in the symptomatic child. Thus, just as the therapist worked hard to establish the parents as the executive subsystem of the family, he or she does well to engage the next most powerful polarity, the identified child patient (Structural Family Therapy).

The therapist should welcome the child to the office and introduce him or herself just briefly. As was the case in engaging the parents in the treatment process, begin the initial meeting for the youngster by asking about *strengths*. Every child has something positive that distinguishes them: sports ability, artistic talents, friends, academic achievement, hobbies, etc. The Self of the child is brought out into the world via these strengths.

Children Are Eager to Share Their Interests and Will Be Soothed by This Initial Conversation

Engagement occurs through the process of recognition and appreciation of another's "goodness." Through this initial conversation, a therapist will also get a quick assessment of verbal ability, intelligence level, comfort with sharing, eye contact, activity level (tolerance for sitting in one place), and other nonverbal indices of anxiety, depression, etc. The Self of the therapist is getting to know and is making room for the Self of the child.

Next, mention to the child that you have met with the parents. Ask the child if she is aware of this and ask what the parents have said about the reasons for coming to a therapist. Ask the child about *her* view of coming to therapy. There is likely a part of the child that resents being there and feels coerced by the parents. The therapist does well to invite the expression of these negative feelings to the surface—all Parts are welcome. It is very important for the therapist to acknowledge and normalize these feelings. This process will be a relief to the child as she experiences the *Acceptance* of her feelings, even if they are about the therapy process itself. In addition, the child will experience an alliance with the therapist for herself and will see that the therapist will not simply be a "hired hand" of the parents, i.e., another adult trying to shape her up and change her. It is important for the therapist to thank the child for being brave enough to talk about these issues. This will begin to set the stage for the therapy process.

Next, ask the child about his life. Generally, this discussion covers three sectors: family, friends, and school. Ask how things are going in each of these areas. The therapist will get a sense of success and struggle from the child's point of view. This will further enhance the process of engagement, as the therapist will have a thumbnail sketch of the child's world. Asking the child about the picture of his nuclear and extended family will also contribute significant data for the therapist in constructing a genogram and contextualizing the presenting problem from a multi-generational perspective (Bowen Theory).

45

Following the discussion covering the important aspects of the child's life, the therapist begins to ask the child about things that are not going so well and what the child would like some help with. A very significant part of this conversation will be the observation of the child's emotional problem-solving style. Is the child an Externalizer: a youngster who will blame his problems on his parents, teachers, siblings, or friends? This usually reflects an overemphasis on Firefighter activity. Or, is the child an Internalizer: placing the locus of difficulties internally, mentioning worry, sadness, somatic complaints, etc.? This usually reflects excess Manager energy. These observations are very significant, as they will orient the therapist to the child's cognitive and emotional style and serve as an indication of family interactive style and structure on the continuum from disengaged to enmeshed (Structural Family Therapy/Internal Family Systems MetaModel). Armed with this knowledge, the therapist will begin to know what kinds of interventions will be most effective for this child and family.

Upon hearing the child's description from his own perspective of his difficulties, the therapist should express appreciation for the child's openness and willingness to express his thoughts and feelings. Again, this sets the stage for the therapy process. It is not necessary for the therapist to make any other responses at this point other than to further engage the child by saying that he or she would like to hear more about this and to be of some help, if that is okay with the child. The child will experience healing as the therapeutic relationship takes hold.

What If the Child Does Not Say Much? What If the Child Has Difficulty Sitting Still?

I have found that welcoming the child into a comfortable and safe treatment setting usually allows them to open up to the therapist. Even the most squirmy or withdrawn children can tolerate 5–10 minutes of verbal discussion. So, I encourage the therapist to try this structure with all child clients. The more traditional (psychoanalytic) approach is to be non-directive and have the child begin the session by choosing some play activity, with the therapist following the child's lead. I feel that this is too open ended, both for child and therapist. There should be some anxiety-reducing opening of a session and a check-in regarding the real world of the child, especially in the assessment phase. Children need to be oriented to the therapy process. Returning to the notion of inoculation to systems thinking, the child will be gently introduced to this approach via brief conversations as described above regarding coming to therapy, describing her world, and discussing problem spots. In addition to engagement in the treatment process and insight into the emotional style of the youngster, this conversation will introduce the process of contextualizing problems, the centerpiece of a systems model.

Having said all of this, it will be important to attend to the child's level of comfort or discomfort with sitting and talking. The therapist should not push the process excessively beyond a child's limits of tolerance. The therapist will need to tune in to the child's nonverbal cues and punctuate the verbal discussion at a particular point and offer to shift to play activity. This is especially true for highly active youngsters. On the other hand, there are overly passive and constricted children who will be perfectly comfortable with sitting for all or most of the session. While this is less of a challenge for most therapists, it will be important to also punctuate the verbal discussion at a certain point and to introduce "activity time" with these youngsters as well. Just as highly active youngsters need to sit and talk, constricted youngsters need to move and do (Sensorimotor Therapy of Patricia Ogden and colleagues). Sampling both sides of children will be enormously helpful diagnostically. Ultimately, seeing both sides of children will likely free them up and foster a more balanced and flexible emotional system, a primary goal of psychotherapy (Acceptance and Commitment Therapy of Stephen Hayes). A child's world can be accessed by a top-down approach, where ideas, words, and thoughts are dominant and can be pathways to deeper emotional experience. On the other hand, a child's world can be accessed by a bottom-up approach, where raw feelings, impulses, bodily sensations, and rhythms are dominant and, with the therapist's guidance, can lead to soothing and gradual articulation (Sensorimotor Therapy).

Activities presented are limited only by the bounds of the therapist's and child's creativity. It is most useful, especially during assessment, to partake in activities that will have a projective element—allowing for an expression of the child's internal experience. The truth is, all play activities have some element of projection that will be revealing to the astute therapist.

I typically will suggest projective drawings in the very first session, especially for youngsters who indicated an interest in artistic endeavors. I have created a therapeutic board game called KidsWorld: Inside and Out, that is a child-friendly play therapy vehicle that taps into a child's experience within the family, at school, and with peers. The game allows the youngster to articulate their worries, sadness, and life experience. This game introduces the IFS approach on a kid's level and builds in exercises and strategies for contextual understanding of their troubles. The child is introduced to the notion of Parts and the game is designed to elicit the child's own curative powers while celebrating their Self. Ample opportunities for expression via thought, action, and mindfulness are available in this game—and all in an atmosphere of fun! (KidsWorld: Inside and Out will be available through the publisher Stoelting Company in the spring of 2014.) For children who seem to need some motoric release, a game of darts or "soft smash" (tennis or basketball with a sponge-type ball) is ideal. Children who are constricted may also welcome a friendly game requiring physical activity.

The therapist should notify the child of the approach of the end of the session as a respectful boundary-making device, so that the child can prepare for re-entry to the outside world. Here, the therapist will sample the child's ability to tolerate limit setting and make note of any difficulties with the important process of frustration tolerance.

It will be important for the therapist to compliment the child on his participation in the session and commend the child on strengths observed in the session. The therapist will discuss plans for the next individual child session and also the plan to have a full-family session in two weeks. Thoughts and feelings about this should be elicited. Most children are pleased to hear about another individual session. Some will be hesitant to embrace the suggestion regarding a full-family session. The child should be invited to discuss his feelings on this matter, which usually encompass worries about being blamed for his problems, inclusion of a disliked sibling, anticipation of sitting without the outlet of activities, etc. Again, the therapist should thank the child for courageously expressing these concerns and let the child know that the he or she will monitor and tune in to his level of comfort or discomfort. It should be noted that while children are given a wide berth of expression of their feelings, the therapist, armed with a clear model of healing, remains in charge. In other words, the child has a vote but does not have veto power—this is ultimately comforting for a youngster.

Always conclude the session on a positive note. It will be likely that the parent will enter the therapy room in order to set the next session and pay the fee. I would invite the child to stay for this brief coda to the session, thereby disallowing some "private" alliance with the parent. Typically, parents will inquire as to the experience of the session. It will be important for the therapist to keep comments positive (mention a strength or two) and be brief. It will also be important for the therapist to allow the child some "space" by normalizing children's desire to talk minimally about the therapy experience. Goodbyes to the parent and child conclude this session.

Session Three: Identified Child Patient

The next session of the assessment phase is for the identified child patient once again. Why do this? Doesn't this focus too much on the individual youngster while de-emphasizing the family context? Another good question.

Seeing the identified child patient is very useful. It reinforces the "face validity," as described above, since the parents will expect the expert therapist to get to know their child. A second session leads to more credibility felt by the parents about the therapist. From the therapist's viewpoint, seeing the child again will afford a wider sampling of her behavior. Children exhibit much variability and sometimes will be on "good behavior" in an initial session and will be more apt to show their less socially appealing Parts in a second interview.

The structure of the second session with the child should be similar to that of the first meeting: 10–15 minutes on "life"—family, friends, school. This will best be followed by a child-oriented activity with room to watch and understand.

Brief preparation for the upcoming family session can be helpful. Asking the child to express feelings and worries about this meeting, topics to raise, etc., can be very useful. Some family therapists may consider this approach as one that feeds into the child's excessive power in the family system. The therapist should monitor this. In reality, the child probably does have disproportionate power on one level and is probably very vulnerable on another level. It should be emphasized that the family session will not be a play-oriented meeting.

Session Four: Family Meeting

At this point, it is likely that the family would have been sufficiently inoculated into a systems approach to the child's difficulty. Both parents have participated as the executive subsystem of the family (Structural Family Therapy). The therapist has been introduced to the experiential world of the parents and the identified child patient (Internal Family Systems MetaModel).

The therapist has set the stage to have them thinking about the larger contexts, in addition to the child himself, as contributory to the presenting problem. Their initial session will have encouraged them to begin hypothesizing regarding the adaptive nature of the problem and at least, spurred a curiosity regarding the Functional Hypothesis. The identified child patient should have some degree of relief that the therapist has now stepped in to deal with the parents and the intensity of triangulation (Bowen Theory) can possibly be diminished. The child patient has experienced the therapist in two sessions as a person available to help him, and not just as an extension of the parental coercive forces (Patterson, 1982) to change and shape up his behavior. The child patient will hopefully begin to feel that there may be alternative solutions to handling an internal and/or interpersonal emotional struggle (even though it is unlikely that the child could verbalize this feeling at this point). The family session should prove to be less anxiety-producing than if it had been conducted without this inoculation.

The family session provides the therapist with a rich store of observations for understanding this particular family system. Though there are common themes among families, each is unique; no story is exactly alike. The therapist will be experiencing the family on verbal and nonverbal levels.

At the outset, it will be helpful for the therapist to greet and spend a few minutes joining with the siblings, as this is their first contact with the therapist. Begin again with an emphasis on their strengths. Asking the siblings what they understand about therapy, and, more specifically, what they know about their parents and brother or sister coming to therapy, can be helpful.

Observing the seating arrangement, activity levels, and spontaneous comments can be of great use to the therapist. This "data" can be quite revealing of family alliances, Attachment patterns, comforting styles, etc.

Next, the therapist does best to ask the parents to take the lead. Once again, this emphasizes the executive status of the parents (Structural Family Therapy). Asking the parents to describe the strengths of their family will again be helpful to create a non-pathologizing climate and to emphasize the health of the family (Solution Focused Model).

The children should be asked, in turn, what they see as the family strengths. I usually move from oldest to youngest in this initial foray. Following the discussion of strengths, I will open the conversation, again looking first to the parents, to questions of problem areas. I will be very vigilant to buffer against this turning into a blaming and scapegoating process of the identified child patient. Usually, at this point in the sequence of sessions, there has been some diminution in this tendency but it still needs to be monitored.

During the discussion of problem spots, I will usually ask some "meta" questions about the family. Examples would be to have family members describe a typical weekday or weekend day in the life of the family (Structural Family Therapy). How do rules get set in the family? Who is in charge? Do the siblings fight more when the parents are home or away from home? How are different opinions discussed? Resolved? How does anger get expressed? Who worries the most? Who worries the least? Is vulnerability allowed? Who are the other significant players in the life of the family—grandparents, housekeepers, etc.? What is the attitude toward the school—respect for its authority or questioning its status? Depending on the answers given, I will linger on one or more of these issues. It is my hope to expose themes and to place the family members in a collaborative mode so that these themes can become the focus, rather than the contentiousness and toxicity that are common at the beginning stage of treatment. Pacing the family, moving from their stated complaints to deeper and more expansive themes, is the stuff of systems diagnosis and will ultimately flow into treatment interventions.

It can be very helpful to suggest a discussion or an enactment (Structural Family Therapy) of a particular problem. For instance, if a child is refusing to do her homework, the therapist may ask the child to talk to her mother, father, or both about this. This process will afford the therapist a rich opportunity to watch what is said, what is not said, what allowances are made for autonomy, who interrupts who, what power dimensions are present, who gives support for the other, if there is any competition, etc.

This is the first opportunity to view the sibling subgroup. Are they supportive of one another? Is there much competition? Are there alliances with different parents? Is there a sibling who looks or sounds very brittle underneath a veneer of the "good child" (not an uncommon occurrence).

The therapist can elicit possible suggestions for dealing with difficulties in this session. The purpose of this is not so much expecting a quick resolution, but to prepare the ground for future problem-solving sessions. For now, the most important process is to foster talking and listening in a respectful manner. The therapist looks for, encourages, and models Self-to-Self interaction. Parts language is introduced throughout the assessment sessions. Beginnings will include unblending family members from their problems and intense reactions to these problems. While this is in the service of assessment, this experience will be very therapeutic for the family (Internal Family Systems MetaModel).

The therapist should conclude the session by mentioning one or two positive aspects that he or she has learned about the family and by making some hopeful statements about the ability of being of help to them. Feedback from family members regarding their experience with the family session can be very helpful.

Session Five: Parent Feedback Session

At this point, the therapist should be able to formulate a Functional Hypothesis regarding the presenting child-focused issue. Having met the key subgroups of the family as well as the family as a whole, the therapist should be able to understand the adaptive nature of the child's symptoms from a systems point of view. The therapist has discussed and heard about the various contexts in which the symptoms are embedded and can now outline some ideas and present feedback to the parents. I will reemphasize that the Functional Hypothesis is not "true" in any absolute sense. It is a hypothesis, a working set of ideas that frames a new understanding for the problems and allows for interventions to flow from this understanding. The Functional Hypothesis can, and usually will, be further refined and shaped over time with the therapist and family working in collaboration. As emphasized in the Common Factors approach and the Contextual Model, all successful therapy involves organizing therapist and clients around a set of beliefs about the nature of the problem. The Functional Hypothesis provides this centerpiece in a powerfully therapeutic manner.

To start the session, eliciting some comments from the parents regarding their experience of the assessment sessions thus far and any thoughts regarding the family session can be useful.

Again, some positive statements about the family are always helpful. Remember, the Functional Hypothesis, at its very nature, is a health-oriented, adaptive view of psychological problems and should be viewed within a picture of family resilience.

Next, the therapist should take the lead in presenting the Functional Hypothesis. Stating it in short bits of information that are digestible, with room for comments and questions, is best. It is crucial to cultivate and maintain a collaborative interaction with the parents.

Examples of the Functional Hypothesis would be:

- Your child's aggression is an attempt to protect against an underlying vulnerability. I noticed that it is a bit difficult to express fear and sadness in this family. I can help with this process by working with you, your child, and the family as a whole.
- Your child's immature behavior appears to reflect a lack of self-confidence. She seems to rely heavily on your management and direction. Now that she is approaching middle school, I can work with her and with you as parents to foster more self-reliance. This will take adjustments and change on everyone's part.
- Your youngster's learning disability has really shaken things up over the past few years for the family. This is one of those "curve balls" that inevitably occur in one fashion or another in the life of a family. Mom's intense involvement, while well intended, seems to actually leave your son feeling like he's a disappointment to you. Coupled with Dad's long work hours and limited availability to spend quality father-son time, your son feels like a failure much of the time. Your son also compares himself to his younger brother, who is a high achiever in school. I'd like to have the opportunity to work on drawing out the strengths in your son, diminishing the worry about the disability that you feel, and easing up the tensions between brothers. I would like to work in combination with you and your son in parent and family sessions. Regular contact with the school will be scheduled.
- Your daughter's stomachaches seem to correspond with worry that she has during the school day. She's very good about talking about these worries. I'd like to create a process in therapy whereby she can tell you more directly what's on her mind regarding friends, school, and the family. It is not up to you to fix these things. I just want you to listen and understand her situation. I will serve as the coach of this process.

It is hoped that these simply put Functional Hypotheses will give the reader a sense of establishing a gentle starting point for fostering greater understanding and joining together with the parents in the treatment process, as well as setting the stage for the subsequent treatment.

The parents are given some time to react to the Functional Hypothesis. They may agree, disagree, and amend parts of what has been presented. Doing this as a team will greatly enhance the therapeutic experience. All are now joined in viewing the problem from a systemic point of view.

The next step is to structure a treatment plan. Since the problem was reframed within a contextual understanding, and since the parents have already experienced the assessment sessions, it will usually not be difficult for the parents to accept and endorse a family approach to treatment at this point. It should be obvious by now that family therapy, in this approach, is a systems model that is a way of *thinking* and not necessarily dictating the number of patients in attendance. Most typically the structure of treatment will encompass a mix of sessions that include individual work for the identified child patient, parent sessions, mother-child, father-child, sibling group, or whole family meetings, depending on what the focus will be. The specific sequence of sessions will be set and easily amended as therapy goes forward, in accordance with the degree of progress.

It is not unusual for a therapist to attempt to move rapidly from child-focused to marital conflict. This is a strategic error. The parents have sought help for their child. Even if they are having blatant conflict and even if they begin to ask for assistance with their marriage, the therapist will do best to begin with a child-focus and to later on re-contract to work with the couple if they so desire. If the jump is made too soon, parents will often resent the movement into another arena. This can be experienced as altering the "script," or mixing metaphors. The therapist will most definitely be doing parent counseling anyway and thereby will be likely addressing marital issues indirectly. The family is a hologram. Accept their point of entry to therapy and your work will reach the level of systems change (Strategic Therapy).

Restating the team approach and reviewing the relevant themes and structure will conclude the parent feedback session. This brings closure to the assessment phase. At this point, when done successfully, the family will have come a distance in being inoculated into a systems approach to their child's problems in the most respectful, empathic, and collaborative manner (Narrative Therapy). A therapeutic alliance now exists as a foundation from which meaningful therapy can take place. The therapist has brought the family from a state of uncertainty and anxiety to a beginning level of understanding via the Functional Hypothesis the challenging aspects (Parts) of their youngster and to feel that they have a trusted ally to help them.

How Do We Assess the Biological Context of Behavior?

Each child is unique. This is true from birth onward. If you've had the experience of peeking into a neonatal unit you will have seen babies who are very fidgety, extremely quiet, and the whole range in between. Some seem to be curious about their surroundings while others seem to be impervious to the activity around them. Some babies cry profusely and others make not a peep. Some of the little ones seem to be easily comforted while some cannot be consoled. From the beginning, there is a plethora of individual differences in traits and temperament.

We see children in our offices with an amazing range of physicality. I have had the honor to work with many, many kids with autism, ADHD, childhood diabetes, epilepsy, motor issues, brain-based learning problems, and so on. What is our role when faced with these biologically based issues? We encounter the whole child. He is not the disorder but he has a condition that constrains his functioning in some way. The therapist is consulted when there is anxiety related to the disorder or unhappiness in reaction to the condition, located internal to the child and/or in the parents and siblings. The way that the family is organized around the symptom is problematic. I have been impressed (and touched) with parents who can stay centered in the face of their child's condition, provide him with the services needed, and feel empathy toward the difficulties. These parents have taught me a lot about the power of Acceptance and the ability to bring Self-leadership to their family.

This is not always the case, however. Parents start with high hopes regarding their children. They often form an idealized image of their child-to-be during pregnancy. Children will inevitably be less than perfect. The degree of "fit" between expectation and reality presents a challenge for parents and children as they grow up (Chess, Thomas, & Birch, 1968; Turecki, 1985). The emotions stirred by discrepancies of fit interact with the degree to which Attachment history is secure for parent and child. The more secure the Attachment history for a parent, the more likely that they will be able to relate to challenges of temperament with empathy. If the Attachment history is insecure or traumatic, there will likely be a surge of anxiety, sadness, and inadequacy (Exiles) that will filter into the emotional and behavioral dynamics between parent and child. The parent feels disillusioned and the child sees disappointment in the eyes of the people most important to her developing self-esteem (Wachtel, 1994). This becomes amplified when two parents become extremely reactive to one another, precipitated by their experience of the child's disorder. The family anxiety further escalates with siblings struggling with the fallout from the tension.

The IFS approach to such situations is to separate the disorder from the person. The disorder is a Part of the child, not his essence or Self. The therapy will be structured around how each family member relates to the disorder. Yes, each person in the family has a significant relationship to the disorder. A key question to ask the child is, "How do you feel toward . . . (e.g., the hyper behavior, the autistic part, the reading disability, the diabetes and so on)?" This allows for an unblending of the Part from Self and will allow the child to be regarded and valued separate from this problem area. It also allows the therapist and client to join together to bring empathy to this Part.

Likewise, the parent is asked if he or she would like some help with the pressure and unhappiness that this problem has stirred up. The therapist can then establish a working alliance with the parents that eventually can re-center them to bring forth Self-energy by which to help their youngster. Repair of Attachment Injury and traumatization can proceed. Work with siblings will also give voice to their struggles and help them to unburden from the weight of experiencing their parents' excessive management of the disorder, seen by the sibling as special attention to their brother or sister, often to the neglect of their needs. Siblings frequently find themselves being in a caretaker role, acting as a social buffer for their brother or sister, experiencing shame in peer relations, etc.

The goal is to be in Self-to-Self relationships among family members. A parallel process is then likely to be fostered as the parents interact with the school. The disability does not go away but it meets with empathy and Acceptance. When met with Self-energy, the child and family become allies, working to help nurture the internal and interpersonal environment.

Does the Assessment Phase Change Structure When Dealing with a Family of Parental Separation or Divorce?

Yes, I believe it's best to alter the structure of assessment when dealing with separated or divorced parents. It will be important for the therapist to convince the parent who makes the initial phone call that involvement of both parents is crucial to the success of the therapy. If there exists much contentiousness between parents, this may be a difficult proposal, especially if the non-custodial parent has minimal contact with the children.

I have found that if the non-custodial parent is not contacted, especially when a contentious relationship persists for the parents, a risk is created that this parent will overtly or covertly sabotage the treatment by convincing the youngster that psychotherapy is a bad thing to do (i.e., the therapy itself becomes fodder for the marital conflict). Without the alliance with both parents, the therapist will be swimming against the current and the treatment will be quite difficult or need to be aborted. If the call-in parent sanctions the contact with the other parent, the therapist can ask if he or she will give the phone number to the non-custodial parent, or, if it is preferred, the therapist can initiate a call to that parent. When that contact is made, emphasizing the importance of both parents' involvement in the treatment will usually allow for a healthy beginning of the assessment process.

In cases of separation or divorce, I would recommend that the therapist meet separately with each parent in order to get started. This structure will guard against the toxicity of the marital strife seeping into the treatment room from the beginning. This way, each parent meets the therapist, forms an alliance, and is engaged in the child-focused exploration. In addition, if the therapist were to meet with both parents together, young children may get a sense that their parents are being reunited, resulting in false hopes feeding into extant fantasies about this process. I think that this is too confusing for children. If successful work proceeds in such cases, it will be very helpful to have joint parent sessions later on, so that the family structure of divorce can be experienced and discussed in a healthy manner. In my opinion, this is too risky a process before building strong alliances with parents and children.

Following separate meetings, the therapist proceeds with two sessions for the individual child patient, as described above. It is best in situations of separation or divorce to have each parent have a session with the child and siblings. Again, by not pushing in both parents together at this early stage, the therapist is respectful and sensitive to the family structure without creating false hopes. These sessions also more realistically reflect the current state of the family, i.e., the children are either with Mom or Dad, not both together.

Following these separate sessions, conducted much the same way as with an intact family, the therapist arranges for separate feedback sessions with each parent. These sessions are also conducted in the same way as described above. The hoped-for goal is that the assessment phase will end with both parents in alliance with the therapist regarding help for their youngster and with the family understanding the adaptive/contextual nature of the symptoms as the therapist formulates a Functional Hypothesis.

Are There Times When the Conflict is Too Intense to Be Successful with This Approach to Families of Separation and Divorce?

Yes. In a small percentage of cases, there is such an adversarial positioning of the parents that therapy itself becomes yet another contentious issue. For the ex-husband, "anything she does is something that I will challenge," or vice versa for the wife.

While the therapist may attempt to work with only the involvement of one parent, it will be crucial to continue to try to engage the other parent over time. In cases when this is not possible, I feel that there will be constraints on the range of therapy that will be accomplished. A choice for the therapist is to suggest that therapy will not work well unless both parents support the process. Such a therapist may state that she will defer the start of the assessment until they can both agree or accept the need for the treatment. The latter option is difficult when one knows that there is a child suffering with emotional turmoil. I have come to feel, however, that this might be the most therapeutic message in the long run. Each family therapist needs to grapple with these choices.

Should There be Special Considerations for Assessments with Families with an Identified Adolescent Patient?

I have usually found that the assessment process as described for child-focused cases works well through age 18. Contrary to popular belief, most teens seem relieved that the therapist will be meeting with the parents and working with the entire family. The structure of the process itself seems to resonate with feelings that the adolescent carries but cannot always articulate, i.e., that his family needs attention and that it is too much pressure for him to be caught in the middle of many conflicting forces. Having a therapist enter the system is the beginning of new options.

Having said this, it can be helpful, particularly with older adolescents, to offer to meet with them prior to the initial parents' session. This gesture respects the oft-stated need for the teen to tell her story without parental coloration or intrusion. I have found that some teens exercise this option while most accept the usual structure with parents being seen for the initial session. Teens will appreciate the offer as a show of respect for their needs.

The above-stated sensitivity to the adolescent's feelings regarding the structure of assessment and treatment cannot be emphasized too much. Inviting the teen to express himself regarding the idea of coming to therapy or being coerced by parents is an extremely helpful way to join with him in the process, even if the discussion is about how he is planning to block or defy the process itself. Remember, the means to the ends are as important (or, in therapy, perhaps more important) as the ends in themselves. This is nowhere more true than in work with adolescents.

Issues of confidentiality may be heightened with teens. Confidentiality implies boundaries and comfort with individuation and connection. In psychotherapy, I view confidentiality as a verb: it cannot be responded to in a yes-no manner. Yes, a healthy family needs to allow for boundaries of privacy. At the same time, excessive pressure to keep parents out or to have children divulge, needs to be understood by the family members. Not infrequently, the process of treatment will be a grappling with these questions and family members will need to "sweat out" bringing such

Parts to be examined. These are key issues for the therapist to keep in mind. An extended discussion of confidentiality can be found in the special Frequently Asked Questions chapter.

With teen clients, the sessions will be largely talk focused. Play material will not be age appropriate, except where there may be a developmental delay or a grossly nonverbal teen who needs to express herself via activities, perhaps art or music. It is usually helpful to invite teens to bring in any creative productions to share as a representation of their self-expression. More time spent on exploration of connection to peer groups will afford the therapist valuable information. For many teens, the peer group is a powerful other "family" (Taffel 2001, 2005). Beyond this, proceeding with the assessment process as described above should be quite effective.

5

ORGANIZING CONCEPTS AND PRINCIPLES FOR TREATMENT OF CHILDREN AND THEIR FAMILIES

The Functional Hypothesis and Acceptance: The Common Factors of the Intrapsychic and Relational Healing Process

As mentioned previously, each family is unique and each symptom picture or problem has a unique set of factors contributory to it. The structure of therapy will typically be a mix of individual child sessions for the identified child patient, parent sessions, mother-child sessions, father-child sessions, sibling sessions, and whole family sessions. Also, when needed, meetings with the family and school personnel or with social service agencies will be part of a systems approach. In certain circumstances, inclusion of extended family will be important. This is the most comprehensive way of treating intrapsychic, interpersonal, and larger systemic issues that form the contexts of the presenting problem. There is a set of useful concepts and processes that will help guide the systems-informed family therapist in treating child-focused issues.

The most important organizing principle flows from the Functional Hypothesis: the problem itself is not the problem. It is how the family arranges themselves around the problem that is the essence and challenge for the therapy. We all face life's traumas, whether due to physical limitations, loss of loved ones, imposition of emotional reactivity from others, abuse from within or outside the family, societal constraints of gender, or issues of race and ethnicity that are contributory to a sense of emotional and/or economic powerlessness, etc. In response to these traumas, the individual and the family system organize to deal with such insults to our body and mind. The individual and family produce survival-based strategies (conscious and unconscious), aimed at dealing with the pain of these traumas. These strategies will work to ease some of the emotional/physical pain. Some strategies will continue to work over an extended period of time. Some strategies will be effective on a short-term basis. There are strategies that work in specific situations.

The difficulty that can arise is that these strategies, initially intended as useful, when overextended, can backfire or create new problems. When this occurs, families call upon a family therapist. They are stuck in cycles of solution-generated problems.

Understanding this process is the essence of the family therapy. Accepting that symptoms have survival-based intentions attached to them will allow the therapist to know the child and family in the deepest and most respectful way. From this process, empathy will flow and healing will occur. If the therapist has difficulty arriving at an understanding of the adaptive nature of symptomatology, he or she must examine the constraints, either internal or external, blocking this understanding. Once these constraints are sufficiently removed, effective therapy can proceed.

For child-focused cases, the therapist will need to inquire about and observe how the symptom itself is an attempt at survival within multiple contexts. The patient or family should not be "rushed" out of their symptomatology until this understanding is achieved and the nature of the problems is appreciated. The therapist's Acceptance, alliance, and curiosity regarding anxiety, depression, and even self-injurious tendencies will communicate the belief in symptoms as attempts at adaptation. Ultimately, this will serve to unburden the emotional systems of our clients.

Next, the therapist needs to work with internal and interpersonal ecologies to allow some room for new learning. Usually this will occur when the adaptive nature of symptoms is appreciated (Internal Family Systems MetaModel).

Parents will need to learn that the child is not being "bad" but is trying to cope. Their attempts at solving the problem, though paved with good intentions, may actually be interfering with the possibility of healing. For instance, when parents try to "shape up" their child, this process may put the child in a defensive position, thereby holding on to their behaviors to protect against the challenge to their autonomy. Instead, parents can be guided to move away from the position of "fixing" their youngster (therapists need to be mindful of this tendency as well), and instead move toward reacting differently to the child's problematic behavior. When faced with empathy rather than blame by parents who let go of coercive strategies, the child will then experience greater degrees of freedom to choose alternative coping strategies under the collaborative guidance of the therapist and parents.

This is the essence of successful child-focused family therapy. All sessions in every combination should flow from this conceptual base. This is what Acceptance is. There are many models currently that are converging on Acceptance (Bach & Moran, 2008; Jacobson & Christiansen, 1996; Mones & Patalano 2000; and Wachtel, 2011). Other models may not overtly emphasize this process, but when they are successful, it is Acceptance that is the Common Factor in healing.

Are There Useful Beliefs in Working with Parents?

Yes. Parents are the most important allies for the child-focused therapist. At the same time, parents are the most important allies for the child. Moving the parents from a blaming or toxic position to one of empathy will be key to the curative process of treatment. Almost always, the therapist is faced with parental Parts that are reactive to the child's Parts, i.e., a Manager confronts a Firefighter, etc.

With good intentions, parents respond to their children's problems with either too much or too little involvement. Both polarities will fuel the maintenance and/or exacerbation of symptoms.

The therapist will help to position the parents in a midrange of reactivity. Helping parents to know their child and to respond to his needs will be crucial. When parents respond in accordance with their own needs, anxieties, sadness, etc., either by imposing their will on the child or by avoidance of intervention, difficulties will persist.

Parents can be coached to clear away blaming, angry, and critical Parts (Internal Family Systems MetaModel). The therapist will appeal to the parents and ask whether they would like to react differently to their youngster. Next, they will be helped to recognize what the child needs, differentiated from the parental expectations. Some parents will struggle with this. It will be hard for them to give up their visions of their child being a top student or a star athlete, etc., and to accept her human, imperfect state. The more narcissistic a parent is, i.e., invested in perfection and image, the more difficult this task will be. The therapist must recognize degrees of struggle with this and be very patient with this process of transformation of the parent. Parents can be helped to see and understand their intense investment in the success of their child, based on their own sense of success and vulnerability and based on the intensity of defense against imperfection. Both over- and under-involvement are really strategies for parental coping with this emotional struggle.

As parents move toward Acceptance and empathy for their child, emotional space will open up and the family system will be supportive of growth and development for all members. Taking ownership for imperfection and striving for the serenity to accept things that are beyond a parent's control is a most powerful curative process.

The goal that needs to be stated to parents is that the therapy will not "cure" the child's ADHD or autism or learning deficits. Therapy will, however, be a very powerful process whereby the child will recognize his strengths and talents and experience Acceptance internally. Concurrently, parents will learn to view their youngster as a lovable person with much to offer the world. The process of therapy in the IFS MetaModel will bring out Self energy in the child as well as the parents so that imperfections, deficits, and the inevitable slings and arrows of life events will be met with compassion, clarity, courage, and creativity. The result will be Self-to-Self interaction within the family, caring for difficulties in whatever form they appear. This transformation will decrease the problem focus and help build healthy, loving interactions.

6

INTRAPSYCHIC TREATMENT OF CHILDREN

Celebrate Self!

The treatment of children will involve a combination of individual child sessions, family therapy sessions, and parent therapy sessions. This chapter will focus on individual therapy sessions with children.

Almost without exception, young children (ages 5–12) are very happy to arrive at my office and enthusiastically go from the waiting room to my consultation room. Why are they excited to travel here, to meet a strange, bearded man for 45 minutes? Yes, the office has some interesting toys and play material, but probably less extensive an offering than most kids possess at home. I like to think of the atmosphere of the therapy setting as acoustic music in a heavy-metal world. It is calm, quiet, unpressured, and noncritical. The child is Accepted as is. Whatever the child says and does, I am curious and supportive. Above all else, the child's Self is celebrated! My Self meets her Self. My Self meets her Parts. It is okay here.

The essence of what happens in our sessions together is to listen carefully for Self-expression and invite it into the room. Most typically Self is expressed and experienced through Attachments and self-efficacy. The process is far more important than content. The child's strengths are invited into the room.

Celebrating Self happens in many ways. The therapist listens closely to what the child has to say. The child can experience that the therapist is there for her. The therapist does not have an agenda for the child other than to heal the Parts that are in pain. The therapist cannot be a "hired hand" of the parents, even though these same parents are paying for the therapist to "shape up" the child. The therapist brings Self-energy (calmness, clarity, curiosity, compassion, confidence, creativity, courage, and connection) to the Parts of the child. The essence of the therapy is to remove the constraints imposed by the child's Protective Parts so that the intact Self-energy of the child can take a leadership position in the child's internal emotional system.

Children express their Selves in many ways. Self is difficult to define. Philosophers and scientists have grappled with this concept through the centuries (Sprintzen, 2009). The IFS MetaModel holds that Self is present from birth. It is a combination of consciousness and survival capacity initially expressed without organized language via motoric, kinesthetic feedback, internally and interpersonally. Globalized sounds of pleasure and distress accompany the expression of Self through body movement. There is awareness that survival depends largely on caretakers. Two forces of growth are present from the start: (1) Individuation, i.e., growing into one's full biological/psychological/spiritual capacity as a seedling grows to full bloom, and (2) Dependency, i.e., needing adults to feed and protect as individuation unfolds, which is as essential as the flower needing adequate sunlight and water. I believe that the child comes equipped with autoimmune mechanisms for physical as well as psychological survival.

Attunement to this child at this time with this set of temperaments allows Self to flourish. Lack of attunement will bring forth defensiveness via Protective Parts and Self becomes constrained. Self often expresses itself via the child's competencies—in art, music, writing, humor, or relating. You can see their bodies relax and engage as their strengths are welcomed out. Another vehicle for Self-expression is discussion of Attachments: Nan, a 14-year-old autistic teen is "obsessed" with Sesame Street characters—she knows the year, episode, and segment when Big Bird, Elmo, Bert and Ernie, etc., appeared teaching a letter, number, life lesson, etc. Her parents want her to stop this obsession, feeling that it interferes with her social development—it is too "babyish." I speak with the parents and tell them that I think that this "obsession" is Nan's lifeline to understanding human interaction and feelings. She is *attached* to Sesame Street—this is how an autistic child relates. These loving parents, at first confused, were gradually able to endorse this idea and allowed for the therapy sessions to welcome this "obsession." Ten years later, Nan, having made great use of this process, has graduated a two-year college in computer graphic arts creating some of her own characters! She still navigates through life with learning from Kermit and Miss Piggy! Yes, there is a Self in autistic youngsters, just accessed in very unusual ways.

The therapist needs always to be operating with the Functional Hypothesis in the lead. Ana tells me about her "hissy fits" that her mother wants her to put an end to (parental Managers). Ana tells me that she hates this in herself (child Managers). I tell her that the hissy fits are saying something important—let's figure this out together. Let's actually be "friends" with the hissy fits because they are trying to help her (survival strategies). I ask her when they happen—usually before sleep or in the morning getting ready for school, or even after she and Mom have had fun together and Mom begins to impose limits and needs to say "no" to her. What are her deeper feelings at those moments?

Ana:	I see in my mind that I will be going to miss Mom at night or at school during the day or that our fun together is ending. I see a picture in my mind that I will be crying—I don't want to cry—next thing I know, I am yelling at Mom.
Therapist:	Wow! Amazing that you know so much about your feelings! So, the hissy fits happen when you try very hard not to be sad. They help you in that way.
Ana:	But they are not good. They make me and Mom upset.
Therapist:	Yes, I see that—maybe we can find a way to let yourself and Mom know about these feelings.
Ana:	Can you tell her?
Therapist:	How about we tell her together? (We bring Mom into the room.) I begin to summarize what Ana has expressed. Ana, strong-willed as always, takes over.
Ana:	"I fight with you but I am really, really sad." Mom is silent and begins to cry. She brings Ana close to her and they embrace. The healing begins.

In IFS language, Ana's hissy fits are not child psychopathology to be punished, controlled, or medicated. They are survival strategies, protecting against the experience of sadness that will be overwhelming for a young child. These Protective Parts have good intentions but have created new problems—adults become exasperated with Ana, feel helpless, or say hurtful things that fuel the cycle to repeat even stronger. The relationship is strained further. Sadness is the Exile that needs attention and soothing with Self-energy. As I extend this understanding to the Protective Part, it begins to give Ana and me some room to meet with and gradually soothe the Exile. This process then extends to the connection of Ana and Mom and then there is sufficient room for Ana to care for her own Exiled feelings of sadness. Healing moves further.

Kiss The Boo-Boo (KTBB)

How do Exiles become healed in children? A child is running in the playground, trips and falls. There is a moment's hesitation, and then the wailing begins. He runs to his father and the father asks where does it hurt. The child, sobbing, points to his elbow; a slight scrape of redness appears. The father, in a very soft voice, says, "Let me kiss the boo-boo," bends down to kiss the elbow, hugs his son, and wipes his tears. The boy runs off to continue playing.

What has happened here? The young child has transitioned from carefree to panic back to carefree within minutes, maybe seconds. The child has become dysregulated, feeling physical pain and likely feeling his vulnerability. He may feel incompetent regarding his physical abilities, embarrassed in public, etc. He knows to come for comforting, receives it, and becomes emotionally regulated again. The father has received him in a non-critical way, accepted his feelings and extended a soothing tone and actions. "I am okay," says the boy to himself. This is an amazingly healing moment.

This same process happens in therapy with children and their parents. The therapist appreciates and accepts the person. The therapist appreciates, accepts and depathologizes feelings, thoughts, and actions that others have viewed as "problems." This process allows the child's emotional system to reorganize, possibly even to reprogram on a neurobiological level. Protective Parts begin to relax and Self-energy shines through, like the sun coming through the clouds. The healing process happens on cognitive, emotional, and physiological levels. Much of IFS psychotherapy is of the KTBB School of treatment!

IFS Play Therapy

Play therapy provides a way for children to express what is inside through games and activities on the outside. Kids are able to introduce us to their Parts through drawing, crafts, board games, storytelling, and physical activities. The possibilities are endless as generated by the creativity of child and therapist.

Sessions will begin with 5–10 minutes of "check-in time," i.e., catching up on the three main spheres of the child's life—family, school, and friends. The conversation is unhurried, without any imposed agenda or content. As important as the content expressed is the tone set by the therapist. The therapist brings forth Self-energy, setting a relaxed pace, quiet tone, and open-hearted reflection, giving the child full attention.

Following the discussion, the child can choose an activity to engage in, selecting from a broad range of material available in the therapy room. The basic structure of play therapy is most helpfully viewed as Self of the therapist joining with Self of the child, focusing on an activity that will provide the externalization of Parts. This structure allows for a therapist-child alliance, creating some distance from Parts to view, understand, and appreciate (Functional Hypothesis) these Parts. It is a way to unblend Parts that is consonant for young children. This is an IFS mode of viewing projective play. It is akin to Michael Mahoney's (2003) reference to the therapist and patient becoming "personal scientists," joining together to explore thoughts, feelings, and behaviors with curiosity and without judgment. Recent research describes how the enactment of emotional communication via concrete external imagery and material is effective in linking body and mind in novel ways, leading to new learning experiences (Kim, Polman & Sanchez-Burks, 2012).

The play activity will bring forth the Parts. Parts can be directly portrayed, as with a child drawing her angry feelings with vivid colors and squiggles. The therapist can simply observe and appreciate such expression and/or ask the child some questions about the drawing—what would she call it ("Angry me"); how does she feel toward it ("I don't like it"); how do your parents react to it ("They yell at me"). I know the usual thing to do is either to yell and scream or just hold the anger in—can we do something a little different today? ("What?"); maybe you and I can talk to the Anger to understand it better ("We can try"). If the child is open to further discussion, she can ask what the Anger needs to say ("They just don't understand me"); what is it that they don't understand ("I'm not sure how to do the math homework"); Do they know about this ("I don't know, probably not"); How would you feel about telling them ("It wouldn't do any good"); so you're angry about their forcing you to do the work and also angry about their wanting you to do well and are not noticing that you may need help with the schoolwork ("Yeah, kinda"); Maybe when you're ready I can help you and your folks to understand this better, maybe even talk together about this ("We can try").

In the IFS MetaModel, it is often the case that the client cannot access deeper Parts. This can be because Protective Parts are blended with Self and experienced as one and the same. This is often the case with kids. Also, their intellectual or developmental level may make differentiation of Self and Parts very difficult. In such cases, the process of Direct Access can be employed, whereby the therapist speaks from his or her Self directly to the Parts of the child. Also, the therapist can speak and interact via play with the externalized Parts represented in play by the child. Much creativity and healing can be expressed in this manner. Krause (2013) has been an innovator in adapting the IFS MetaModel to use Direct Access in the healing of children and to use play material as an externalization of Parts.

Or, if it be the case that the child says, "I don't know" or "I don't want to talk about this," the therapist simply notes this and Accepts it as where the child's internal emotional system is currently situated. Often we must wait until the child's Manager Parts feel safe and ready to step back. As the therapist feels that the child is ready, talking to the Manager Part can begin an important therapeutic conversation. The Manager can be asked the Constraint Question (Breunlin, 1999), "What would it worry would happen to you if you did talk about this?" This question is safer than going directly to content. It can relax Manager Parts and sometimes allow for access to Exiles.

In addition to Parts being directly portrayed as above, they can be elicited during various therapeutic board games. For instance, a youngster selecting a card from the author's enjoyable KidsWorld: Inside and Out Board Game (forthcoming) may talk about " a time when a boy was not picked to be on a team. . . ." Here the therapist could ask about the child's feelings, likely drawing out Exiles, as in "the boy felt very sad." Going a bit further, the therapist can ask what the sad feelings need from the child (Self): how can they be comforted. At times, further conversations about how the child may handle the sadness, such as eating a bunch of cookies (Firefighters), and how those strategies help at the moment but does not really help the sadness in the long term. Again, Acceptance of all answers is important with gentle questions bringing forth Self-energy in the service of healing the Exile.

Another way that Parts can be accessed is via the therapeutic relationship during the activity. A boy chose to play checkers with me. At a certain point, the boy could see that he was not heading for a win. He became jittery and distracted and tried to "change the rules" in his favor. This behavior was clearly an avoidance of feelings of inadequacy and vulnerability. I said that this was always the hardest time in a game and in other situations (the child would not tell his parents when he received a poor grade in school). The Constraint Question was asked: "What do you worry would happen if you just felt these uncomfortable feelings? What do you worry your parents would think if you brought home the low test grade? How would your sister react if this happened?" Useful healing discussions can follow when the therapist has clarity about the emotional location (i.e., what Part am I speaking with?) of the interaction.

It can be very helpful to introduce "quiet time" into the sessions as needed. Many children will respond to breathing exercises as ways to calm their inner systems. Showing a child how to slowly and steadily breathe in through the nose and out through the mouth can serve to self-soothe. This can be applied to activated Parts or can just be a regular exercise to use in the session or at home. Just allowing the breath to be the focus can help the child be "in" a Self-state. This simple process can increase a child's self-efficacy in regulating the activity within their body and in setting up a "window of tolerance" as described by Ogden and colleagues (2006) in Sensorimotor Therapy, allowing the child to navigate between states of hyperarousal and hypoarousal. Mindfulness exercises are presented in a fun way in the author's board game, KidsWorld: Inside and Out.

What Part Does Play Therapy Serve in Child-Focused Family Therapy?

As mentioned previously, family therapy is a way of thinking, specifically a way of thinking systemically and applying the contextual model to understanding a problem. Family therapy does not dictate *who* shall participate in sessions. The therapist will decide whom to invite to each session as a *strategy or vehicle* for healing. In my practice, all combinations of family members will likely be participating in therapy: parents, mother-child, father-child, siblings, and the individual child patients.

While some models, most prominently some practitioners of Bowen Theory, claim that work with parents will be sufficient to help resolve child problems, my own experience and beliefs lean toward viewing the child as a person in need of therapeutic attention, sometimes with his or her family members and sometimes in individual sessions. I have found that children benefit from the therapeutic relationship, especially as family life has become so pressured and rushed. Children need to express their worries and their sadness and need an unburdening process much like adults (Internal Family Systems MetaModel).

In working with a child, I continue to be impressed with children's natural tendency to enter the therapy office finding comfort and meaning in expression via play, transforming the office into a natural habitat for communication and healing. Play therapy is an excellent vehicle by which children from ages 5–12 express themselves. I have found that treatment of preschoolers, following the Assessment phase, is most effectively done via parent training and guidance. Therapy for teens will typically be predominantly conducted through verbal interchange. Exceptions will occur with precocious preschoolers and also with emotionally immature and developmentally delayed teens.

At times, the family therapist faced with child-focused treatment will wonder about the choice of play techniques. In the paragraphs below, I will list my favorites. Please note that any type of play can be a vehicle for projective play. The only bounds are the limits of imagination of the therapist and youngster.

I stock my office with the following play material: crayons, markers (washable), construction paper, sketching paper, modeling clay, hand puppets (family characters, passive-type and aggressive-type animals), building materials (Legos, blocks), cassette tape recorder, small vehicles (cars, trucks, airplanes), chess set, checkers game, several therapeutic board games, books of riddles, books of facts, trivia games, academically oriented games (reading comprehension, math, etc.). My office has a cabinet that opens to a chalkboard and bulletin board. Hangman and playing school and quiz games are favorites in this corner. I also supply some gross motor activities such as darts (plastic, safe), ring toss, a mini-basketball game, etc. I keep a box of stickers, small activity books, and attractive pencils as occasional giveaways to children (especially young ones) for birthdays and special occasions. When kids go away for the summer months to camp, vacation spots, etc., I will present a small gift, which I find serves as a thoughtful transitional object and is a token of well wishes for an experience of self-efficacy.

Each play activity has many levels of therapeutic expression. A checkers game can serve as a quiet vehicle to relate while talking (or not talking), a game to examine and build upon a child's self-esteem, a focal point for working on low frustration tolerance, a game to see how a child handles rules and structure, a game that works through competitive feelings, a game of aggressive "war" contained on a checkerboard, a game for handling fairness and kindness or working through "cheating" and coercive tendencies. The attunement of the therapist will dictate the direction of any of the play activities.

My own style of play is to allow space for the child's expression. I tend to ask questions and give limited interpretations. When I do interpret, I will ask the child if he or she would like me to comment. I find that most child patients have enough "interpretation"/coercion in their lives from parents, teachers, siblings, and peers. Having space to express themselves in play sessions in combination with other more talk-oriented family sessions will be most curative. Instead of interpretation, the IFS MetaModel allows for Direct Access as described above—the Self of the therapist will communicate directly to a Part of the youngster. Modeling in this way can foster this process so that the child will gradually experiment in trying this internally, Self making contact with Parts.

Kinetic Family Drawings: Ask the child who likes to draw to create on a white, unlined paper, "a picture of everyone in their family, including (his/her)self, doing something." This activity consistently produces grist for the therapeutic mill. The therapist can learn a lot about the child's perception of his family from these drawings and from a brief discussion about the picture with the child.

Mutual Storytelling Technique: This technique, created by Richard Gardner, MD, is an ideal child-oriented vehicle for expression. In my own version of this game, the child is invited to be on a TV show for kids, "The Make-Up-A-Story Show." I will be the host and will introduce the child as the "special guest" of the show, who will be invited to tell a story with a beginning, middle, and end that provides a moral (or lesson) for kids of the same age. This game gives the child (and therapist) an opportunity to "ham it up" a bit and allows the child to pull feelings together in an expressive manner. The therapist can ask some questions from the "audience" and also tell a story him or herself, if wanted (Gardner, 1976).

Therapeutic Board Games: Board games such as the Talking, Feeling, Doing Game (Richard A. Gardner, MD), the Ungame, etc are simple, child-oriented vehicles that provide a structure for a therapeutic conversation on important topics. Most children find these games sufficient motivational devices to talk a bit, maintain control of the flow of exposure, and plainly have fun in a relationship with a caring therapist who also can share his or her ideas and be a "real" person in measured, therapeutic doses. These games also have the advantage of "face validity," i.e., they fit the concept of "talking about problems" that children (and their parents) expect from treatment sessions. Newly created by this author, the board game KidsWorld: Inside and Out is a play therapy vehicle that allows youngsters to experience the IFS Stoelting Co. MetaModel and mindfulness exercises in a fun context (forthcoming, 2014).

Office Sports Games: It is helpful to have on hand several gross motor outlets for children that are safe and scaled for on office environment. In my office, a game of (plastic) darts is a favorite. The game can be a stand-up activity to lower the intensity of sit-down discussions for children, a tension-reliever, a self-esteem booster, a child-to-therapist relationship enhancer, an indirect way to show, build, and talk about math skills (tabulating the score), a vehicle for demonstrating aggression or passivity, and a channel for handling competition and frustration tolerance. Other similar outlets include mini-basketball, soft-smash (Nerf balls) paddle ball, ring toss, bean bag catch, etc. Activities involving the body can serve as good vehicles to allow for "bottom-up" access to kids' feelings and thoughts (Sensorimotor Therapy).

Intellectual Skills Games: Also useful are games that challenge a child's skills in academically oriented activities. A trivia game geared toward the appropriate grade level can help children to demonstrate their knowledge or to work thorough their vulnerabilities regarding intellectual limitations. A solid sign of progress within the therapeutic process is when a child selects an activity that is not necessarily his or her arena for strength. Other, similar choices are a reading comprehension board game, or a hangman (spelling skills) game that can also be extended to projective storytelling by constructing short stories using the words that are spelled. Recently the popularity of the TV show, *Who Wants to Be a Millionaire* has spawned spinoffs in many therapy sessions. At times, a child will bring in some homework to show me, and I am glad to witness their work skills and answer questions or respond to comments regarding emotional aspects of this major task of childhood.

Arts and Crafts: There are endless possibilities of creative expression in using markers, construction paper, scissors, glue, etc. Legos and building blocks are timeless favorites for many children. These are wonderful vehicles for projective play and building a therapeutic relationship. Each therapist and each child will be comfortable with certain media and be "teachers" to each other. A wonderful collection of child-friendly activities and interventions has been the contribution of Stern (2002).

Expression Through Music: For young teens in middle school and high school who spend lots of time listening to music, inviting them to bring in their favorite songs on their iPod can be a joining strategy and also give the therapist a sampling of what the youngster is filtering through her head on a daily basis. Asking about "the message" or "the mood" of a song can lead to revealing discussions with this age group.

Emotional Expression Through Writing: I frequently encourage children to keep a journal of their activities that includes a commentary with their own thoughts and feelings. This is a natural extension of therapy and encourages Self-development and expression. Whether or not they share any of this material (usually small bits) is not so relevant. It is a wonderful device (for many adults too) to sort out one's life experiences over time.

Dream Work: Some children will be fascinated by their dreams. If they are interested, I am happy to listen. I am not so much interested in major interpretations, though at times important themes will leap out from the dreamscape and provide clarity for the child and therapist. Again, I see the sharing of dreams as part of a general process of inquiry into the inner world of a young person and to help them appreciate the fascination of the workings of their minds.

At times, children will bring in some of their own choice games from home. While sometimes this can be an avoidance of talking, the skilled therapist will allow some time with this material and weave the activity into a meaningful discussion. The past decade has brought with it an explosion of computer games. While I'm sure that these too can be tools for emotional expression, my preference so far is for low-tech choices. Today's kids are overstimulated by a barrage of TV and electronic-oriented gadgets, the effects of which we are all watching with regard to brain development as well as to the impact on relationships and social intelligence.

As mentioned earlier, I view therapy as providing a quieter place with a softer interaction. I do think that children respond favorably to this "oasis." I do remain open-minded to new devices, however, and there have been some meaningful conversations jump-started with electronic material brought to the session, such as music interests and apps ranging from word puzzles to violent video games.

The common thread woven through all of these techniques is celebrating the Self (Internal Family Systems MetaModel) of the child. The therapist accepts the child and all of his Parts. He is trying to cope and the strategies (symptoms) are appreciated. The Self of the child is there, always, but often constrained by these Protective Parts. Therapy allows the Self to gradually and safely shine through as constraints are removed. I have seen this process time and time again with children of all types, all degrees of intelligence, and all symptom pictures. Children thrive as the warmth of the individual therapy comingles with the depathologizing process of parents, siblings, teachers, etc.

Children can be unburdened (Internal Family Systems MetaModel) from sadness, fear and feelings of inadequacy as the family system shifts to Acceptance and reduces blame, and as parents are more centered themselves. This reverts the family system to a fertile ground that can nurture the goodness within.

Working with Manager Parts of Kids

Therapists on the "front line" in clinics, hospitals, agencies, and private practice know that each child is an individual entity. The same is true for each family. The internal and relational world of a child is unique, something like human fingerprints—while there can be great similarities, and on first encounter there may be a thought that "I've seen this before," no two are exactly alike. This can make our jobs daunting endeavors. Having said this, I believe that it can be very useful to organize one's thinking around certain symptom presentations and family structures.

Children present a tendency to organize their emotional and interpersonal worlds by either internalizing or externalizing. The IFS MetaModel serves as an effective map to track these tendencies and to shape children in families to be more flexible and adaptive.

While every child and family have their own "story," on an internal level we learn that underneath the many presenting problems are feelings of anxiety, depression, shame and inadequacy (Exiles). Protective Parts come in the form of Managers and Firefighters (Quick Fix).

Managers will help to keep us in control and functioning successfully in the world. These Parts are working hard, sometimes around the clock, to keep us from feeling negative feelings.

This works well to some extent, but eventually the overuse of Managers limits psychological flexibility, and the underlying feelings go unattended and are carried as burdens in the child's mind and body. Managers can mask the unwanted feelings. The feelings remain, needing healing.

Hank was a very high achiever in school. He was referred because he cried at home and school on a daily basis. His "strategy" for coping was to push himself to read extra chapters, write extra reports, join the junior swim team with grueling practices and practice his clarinet for long periods of time. When asked by teachers and parents why he cried so much, Hank replied, "I just have to do my best, and when I don't, I get sad."

I let Hank know that the sad Part of him was welcome in my office. He did not have to feel pressure to stop. On the contrary, I wanted to get to meet this Part of him and to see if it needed some help from us. Hank quickly was comforted by this Acceptance and reversal in pressure he was feeling to block the sadness. I worked with his teacher and school counselor to create some time in his school day when Hank could take a short break from class to privately express how his day was going and to cry as needed. This removed the social stigma of his behavior while allowing room to express his feelings. I worked with the parents who initially were wanting a quick stop to the crying, but who could understand the Parts concept and the need for the sadness to be accepted. I could see that the parents carried their own emotional burdens and noted to myself potential work with them in the future.

The work with Hank centered on his telling me of his successes in academics, sports, and music. We made lists (externalized) of worries, mostly around upcoming tests, concerts, and swim meets. Sometimes, worries expressed concerns for his father never knowing his parents and growing up in an orphanage in the Middle East. This loving child seemed to be carrying a legacy (intergenerational) burden of sadness. Hank would do well in games of checkers, chess, etc., in the office. Inevitably when he saw that I was winning or that he made an error in strategy, he tended to change the rules so that he could regain the upper hand. I accepted this over many sessions and one day introduced my "noticing" a Part that was uncomfortable with losing. Hank acknowledged this. We had identified, in a safe manner, a very active Manager.

Over future sessions, I would gently notice the presence of the Manager and knew how important it was to Hank in trying to keep sadness and worry about losing away from him. He could tell me that the Manager was in his head and that the sadness was in his heart and chest. We had a physical reference point and I could periodically check in with his head and heart.

Hank's parents were supportive of his participation in therapy and would attend periodic parenting meetings following the initial assessment phase. This was a powerfully child-centered family. A younger sister was "an annoyance" to her brother, but clearly they were quite loyal to each other. The father, hesitant at first to have his prized son in treatment, became extremely fastidious about scheduling and keeping the sessions constant. The parents, clearly carrying their own burdens, opted to keep the focus on Hank and it worked. Over time, the crying tapered. Eventually, Hank could talk about "not doing so well" on an exam, or not being an Olympic-level swimmer. A wonderful sense of humor began to include the Self-Acceptance of his human fallibility. This gentle, sensitive boy had grown to be a successful, gifted, and self-assured young adolescent.

The work with Hank was essentially appreciating the Manager trying to block the experience of sadness and inadequacy and the Acceptance of intense feelings in Exile. For the IFS therapist, patience is the key to work with Managers. Never waver from the knowledge that the emotional system of the child is protected by the Manager Parts, and know that Managers will wait (sometimes for a long time) until all seems safe. Once that happens, they can step aside, experiment with the child feeling his feelings, and see that he will be okay, he can survive, and that the family system will stay safe and thrive.

In doing work on healing intrapsychic and relational levels, it is best to begin with gaining access to Managers. These Protective Parts often serve as the "gatekeepers" of the internal emotional system and, as such, can block or allow entry of the therapist to this system. The Managers will need to feel safe, appreciated, and accepted by the therapist and client before being able to unblend from Self. Once this process begins (and at times needs to be repeated), the system becomes open for exploration. Likewise, on the relational plane, it is best to focus initially on parental Managers. Worried or critical Parts of a mother and father need to be acknowledged and appreciated as well intentioned in the service of guiding their kids towards success. As an alliance grows between Self of the therapist and parental Protective Managers, the therapist will be more likely to gain access to the internal and relational systems. Once appreciated, the gatekeeper can become an enthusiastic ally in the process of healing. When the therapist feels stuck, it is likely that a Manager is expressing lack of trust in allowing the experience of painful emotions. It will be very helpful for the clinician to be sensitized and mindful of this situation. As therapists grow into their ability to detect Parts, the treatment is enhanced.

Working with Firefighter Parts of Kids

In contrast to children who over-Manage their negative feelings (but just as tenacious) are Firefighter Parts, or quick fix methods of soothing or blocking feelings of anxiety, depression, shame, and inadequacy.

Firefighter Parts tend to be action-oriented ways to distract kids from feeling. These Parts have an immediacy to them, putting out a fire within. As with Managers, while the Firefighter Parts accomplish their mission of dousing out the uncomfortable and painful affect in the moment, the feelings remain in Exile form and are left unattended and unprocessed.

Irma, age sixteen, was a jumble of Firefighter Parts. She stayed out late, drinking and smoking pot, at times experimenting with psychedelic drugs. She may have been having unprotected sex and choosing random partners. There was some history of cutting herself. Not surprisingly, she was drawing Manager responses from parents and school officials. I was called to get her to stop this behavior. The last thing that she needed was a therapist who would be another Manager in her life. She didn't especially want to be in therapy, but she did show up each week.

In situations such as this, it is a challenge for the therapist to stay in Self, and especially hard to harness the courage needed to sit with the Firefighter Parts, but this is powerfully needed and is essential to the healing. If this is not done, the patient will be in a polarization, her Firefighter to the therapist's Manager, in a Parts-to-Parts interaction that is unproductive.

I listened carefully to Irma talking about her life. She had had her foot on the accelerator ever since entering her teens. Her parents had a high-conflict marriage, and she had been exposed to intense fighting throughout her childhood. She was interested in learning but was restless in school.

She found some comforting in her peer group "family." Her sister, three years younger, was low key in manner and a good academic performer. Irma enjoyed writing and was able to express her Self well and I encouraged this. She periodically brought a poem or story in for me to read. Irma's parents were in a toxic recursive cycle with her. They battled with her Firefighter Parts. As is typical, these Parts amplified in response to this.

There was considerable pressure on me from parents and school regarding referrals for medication and thoughts of residential treatment placements. I held steady and was able to slow down the home battles a bit.

Irma gradually saw me as an ally. She was comforted by the fact that I did not aggressively challenge her, though over time I did speak directly to the Firefighter Parts regarding their loyalty to Irma, opining that their overworking was backfiring and blocking Irma's path to growing and individuation. While I didn't battle the Firefighters (this does not work), I did confront them regarding placing Irma in danger and knew that they did not want this. There were many, many crises along the way. The parents became more accepting of Irma and calmed their reactivity of Manager and Firefighter Parts. Gradually, their coercion and anger shifted to greater compassion, and they were okay with Irma choosing an alternative direction to her life's journey. She managed to graduate high school and got a job at a local music store. Eventually, she enrolled in a two-year college, taking writing courses.

Irma's parents' involvement shifted from parent counseling to marital therapy as Irma stabilized. This also included trauma work with the Mom regarding abusive family-of-origin experiences, including sexual molestation. The father admitted to his secret addictive tendencies (frequent pot smoking), and we began some work on this. He decided to participate in Narcotics Anonymous. A younger sister consulted with me as she struggled with some peer issues. I anticipate that treatment will continue intermittently with this family.

7

HEALING ATTACHMENT
INJURIES OF CHILDREN

Attachment Issues in Kids

There are treatments where the trajectory of treatment gets stuck, even when attention is being paid over and over again to Manager and Firefighter Parts. This does not mean that the model is not effective. In my experience, it probably means that the Parts are not feeling safe enough to make room for Self-energy. While to some extent this drama occurs in all cases, when particularly tenacious it is because the Parts do not feel that there will be reliable Attachment experiences available should they step aside. In their way, the Parts have become internal parent figures. While far from perfect and often generating a new set of problems, the Parts have become reliable and predictable in a world where parents and other adult figures just cannot be trusted. This occurs in children where their basic caretaking needs and rights have been violated.

This can be experienced in cases of physical abuse, sexual abuse, and exposure to parents who are either too withdrawn to be emotionally available or immersed in their own mire of Parts, especially Firefighters.

In such cases, Self-energy will be blocked. The healing will occur via the reparative aspects of the therapeutic relationship interwoven with gradual and careful Parts work. As the therapist's Self is a constant and persistent force, the client's Parts will begin to allow the light of the client's Self to peak out from behind the clouds. This is a beautiful process to behold.

Unburdening Children

In the IFS MetaModel, healing comes in two modal places: first, the process of Acceptance and welcoming of the person and her symptoms. Viewing symptoms as adaptive and survival based is crucial, applying the Functional Hypothesis as emphasized throughout this book. The second process involves the experiencing of Exiles in session, witnessed by Self of the therapist and Self of the client. In these powerful therapeutic moments, long-held sadness, shame, guilt, and inadequacy are brought into awareness and are accepted and nurtured by Self-energy.

These feelings are welcomed into the present tense in a safe and reassuring environment. This is a "kiss the boo-boo" moment. Overwhelming emotions are soothed and met with loving Self-energy. It can be very powerful to create a ritual for some clients. The ritual can be a letting go of the residue of trauma by sending the painful emotions, memories, and injuries away into the light, over the horizon, up in smoke, by breathing them out, etc.—the varieties are endless.

How much of this process is possible for kids? As we have seen, the empathic setting of our sessions is powerfully therapeutic for children. They can experience the Acceptance of their Protective Parts and lift constraints on Self. Self now has greater degrees of freedom. Can children go further? Can they unburden the emotional pain and sadness that they carry? I would say yes, but it is more complicated than with adults.

Children are currently living in their family context. So, while they may experience the safety and freedom to be in Self and have painful feelings witnessed in their therapy sessions, they are embedded in their family. Protective Parts will step back sufficiently only if it is safe enough—if the context permits. The context is their family. They will require a critical mass of Self-led parenting in order for their own emotional system to risk unburdening. I have seen the lifting of burdens, but only when Self of the therapist meets the Self of the child, the Self of the therapist has met the Self of the Parents, and parents and children have been able to relate in a Self-to-Self manner. Then it will be safe for the child to unburden Exiles.

It should be noted that Unburdening does not need to be a dramatic moment. At times, the process of befriending of Protective Parts leads to Acceptance, allowing for Unburdening to happen naturally and spontaneously. In other instances, the regularity and constancy of the client-therapist relationship provides a gradual and steady letting go of stored emotional pain. Mostly, what I have observed is a lifting of worry, sadness, shame and feelings of inadequacy when the parent-child relationship transforms from one of coercion, disappointment, and blame to one of compassion and Acceptance. Finally, youngsters can feel safe and appreciated for the gift that they are. The Self is now able to shine through in so many ways.

8

GUIDING THE PROCESS OF SELF-LED PARENTING

As mentioned above, the ultimate healing for children will come when their behavior, feelings, and who they are is met with Acceptance by their parents. How is a conflict-laden, Parts-to-Parts relationship transformed to a Self-to-Self interaction?

Part of IFS treatment with kids will need to be IFS work with parents. In its essence, work with parents will take away the frustration, hopelessness, and inadequacy that parents feel and guide them to a compassionate and competent parenting position. A key question to ask the parents during the initial assessment sessions is, "While I work on helping your child feel better about herself, would you like me to help you not feel so stressed by the issues, reduce your sense of powerlessness, and improve your daily life while your child is still struggling?" Most parents will agree to this. They want to feel better. (They too want to be healed.)

Armed with this contract with the parents, a parallel track of treatment is now established. The therapist will now begin to meet with the parents once or twice monthly. Parents will now be able to be received with the same process of Acceptance by the therapist. The therapist will have greater credibility as he or she is meeting regularly with their child.

IFS Parent sessions will begin by identifying the Parts that carry frustration, Parts that are rigidly applying Manager energy to themselves and their child, and Parts that promote quick-fix analgesics as Firefighters in their daily lives.

Ana's mother, Blanche, was relieved to have the opportunity for a monthly parent session. As mentioned, she looked exhausted after a non-stop day of work and parenting her high-energy, strong-willed daughter. She craved her favorite escape, reading romance novels (Firefighter). Any time she would sit down to read in the evening, Ana would appear doing calisthenics or bringing projects for Blanche to join in on. Blanche tried hard to respond supportively to her daughter but the metacommunication was "please go away . . . I need this time for quiet relaxation . . . please don't interrupt my private time. . . ." This nonverbal message was received by Ana as rejection, especially when she craved the closeness with her mom.

An early discussion had us look at the different styles and different energy exuded by her and her daughter. We talked about the different temperaments that exist in the biological sphere for mother and daughter. No blame, just what is a default position—this is the parent-child package in this particular family.

We looked at the "clash" of these styles without labeling them as either "good" or "bad." Blanche immediately relaxed during these conversations. I believe that I was reaching and comforting her feelings of inadequacy. I allowed her to pause and linger on this sense of relief. When, in a mother-daughter session, she experienced (see Chapter 6) Ana's admission of missing her and carrying underlying sadness prior to erupting into hissy fits, the anger melted away and she began to see beyond Ana's oppositionalism. Ana was no longer "bad," she was just "sad." Blanche had no problem in generously comforting the sad Part of Ana.

In response to Ana's courageous disclosure of sadness, Blanche began to talk about her own sadness and feelings of inadequacy as a person. She talked about her choice of marital partner, Charlie, who was a "nice bright guy with a severe alcohol problem." Her pregnancy with Ana was rife with fights with Charlie, who would arrive home in a drunken stupor and frequently have rageful Parts triggered at home. It was at this time that I suggested that Charlie, Ana's father, be part of the treatment. Blanche was initially cautious, then glad to have this arrangement, realizing that Ana will of course have a lifelong relationship with Charlie. Charlie agreed to sessions as often as allowed by his mandated inpatient rehabilitation program.

Blanche went further in her sessions and connected the sadness about her aborted marriage to struggles throughout her life with her father, who was a severe alcoholic himself, dying of complications of this disease. Conflict-laden experiences with her mother were also explored.

Blanche allowed access to her Exiles in our sessions. As I brought my Self-energy to her injured Parts, she did the same. As her Exiles were accessed, healing began and Managers relaxed internally and were less in play in parenting Ana. In another mother-daughter session, Ana actually suggested that her mom can read a book while she plays nearby as part of the evening routine at home. Blanche became more open to the possibility of forming healthy new attachments to men and began dating, cautiously, then with greater courage and confidence. Ana, also cautious at first, became very enthusiastic about the possibility of a stable, loving family.

The reader can see how shifts occur in the treatment and how a conflict-laden mother-daughter interaction converts into a relationship of Acceptance of differences, allowance for sadness and emotional pain, and release of constraints on the compassion of Self-to-Self energy.

The most important goal of work with parents is to help guide them to a Self-led position. As they can let go and unburden their own Exiles of sadness, anxiety, shame, and feelings of anxiety their core loving nature rises to the dominant position intrapsychically and can then be extended to the important people in their lives. As we saw in the previous chapter, this transformed internal experience provides the grounding for children to bask in the glow of parental Acceptance and compassion, allowing for the safety of secure Attachment and leading to their own process of Unburdening.

9

WORKING WITH SIBLINGS

Psychological theories and models of psychotherapy have consistently emphasized the importance of parent-child interaction in the understanding of personality development. However, with some rare exceptions (Adler, 1927; Bowen, 1978; Minuchin, 1974; Sherman & Dinkmeyer, 1987; Sulloway, 1996; Toman, 1976, 1988), most models have overlooked the tremendous impact of sibling relationships throughout the many phases of the life cycle. Except for the time spent together by spouses in long-term marriages, cumulative time spent with siblings during the formative years far surpasses time in any other relationship during our lifetime. As is the case between parents and children, siblings, by definition, are permanently bound, with no escape, to their familial positions.

It is within sibling interactions that children learn to deal with differences, fairness, sharing, and conflict. Sibling experiences are the original "learning laboratory" for self-growth while sharing resources of love, attention, and discipline from parents. Processes of power, gender identity, competition, cooperation, affection, proximity-distance, communication, and empathy are regularly negotiated between and among brothers and sisters. The reader will note that this list of experiences and more are the same items that will ultimately make or break our relationships with peers, colleagues, and most potently our intimate partners (Mones, 2001).

There are several key themes that weave through sibling interactions that we can link to the formation of Exiles and Protective Parts observed in our work with children.

Complementary Role Development. For the most part, siblings are engaged in sharing physical and psychological space within families. While parental influence and societal expectations of gender and birth order play key roles in how our Self gets defined, there are key connections to our identity formation within our sibling bonds (Bank & Kahn, 1982). The vast majority of siblings have complementary relationships emanating from a non-shared environment, that is, the family climate that one child is born into has significant experiential differences from the climate that other siblings are born into. Dunn and Plomin (1990) make a convincing argument regarding this fact based on sophisticated analyses of behavioral genetics. Like pieces of a puzzle, a brother may be "the athlete" and "the shy one" while his sister is "the scholar" and "the assertive one." Siblings appear to share emotional space, dividing up the psychological territory of who they are and what they believe, much as they share the physical space within the home.

The IFS MetaModel is largely about lifting constraints on Self-leadership. Managers and Firefighters tenaciously protect us from psychological pain. Much of our treatment involves understanding the survival nature of these Protective Parts (Functional Hypothesis) and gradually providing safety for these Parts to step back. As this process occurs, Self-energy has a greater degree of freedom and takes its rightful leadership position. Now, the healing of Exiles is possible as Self can Accept and move towards the pain as the therapist bears witness.

As mentioned above, siblings constrain one another. There appears to be a zero-sum game at play—if I am extroverted, my brother is introverted, if I am responsible, he is immature, and so on. Bringing the sibling relationship into the therapy can lead to understanding one another, diminishing the polarization between siblings, and ultimately lifting constraints and allowing Self-energy to shine through.

Sibling work can be done with the identified child patient expressing his feelings toward his brother or sister. Even more powerful an intervention is inviting siblings to meet together. In these sessions it is possible to redirect fierce conflict into empathy, teamwork, and growth.

Dan, a teen diagnosed with Asperger's Syndrome, is the identified patient and is grappling with social awkwardness and feelings of ostracism with peers. After a few sessions, he states, "Do you want to know my biggest problem? My brother." Dan goes on to tell me that his brother, two years his junior with learning problems of his own, taunts him with frequent putdowns regarding his habits of repetitive talk, sloppy eating style, and obsessions with drawing ships and planes. He (and his parents) readily granted me permission to meet with his brother Eddie. In his session, Eddie expressed great frustration with Dan and his parents' inordinate attention to Dan's special needs, and his social embarrassment in being Dan's brother. "I know that I am cruel to him, but he drives me crazy," Eddie exclaimed with tears in his eyes.

Both brothers, when asked, were eager to meet together. This session was quite touching. I asked them to have the frustration and anger step back and to really talk to each other. They took turns and took off quite expressively. Each in turn expressed sadness regarding their struggles with learning and social status. As it turns out, Eddie felt deeply for Dan's limitations and actually feels quite protective of his brother. Dan was all smiles to learn of his brother's love and concern. You could feel the burdens lift! They came up with several ideas that would buffer their clashes, including a weekly bowling session where they would review the events of the week and pledge to help each other with challenges that occurred. As the session wound down the brothers spontaneously hugged one another. We agreed to frequent sessions to talk together and build on the strengths of this sibling bond.

The complementary nature of sibling relationships and resultant impact on constraining Self plays out in so many ways in our lives. Our ability to be close or distant from others is powerfully influenced by the safety-risk dimension set forth in our sibling interaction. Our grappling with fairness and justice is greatly affected by the degree of success in negotiating with our siblings throughout our formative years. Being able to grant forgiveness for misdeeds and injustices along with apologizing for hurts that we impose unto others is influenced by our experience with our brothers and sisters. Dealing with the power and hierarchy inherent in peer relationships and dealing with authority figures will have strong roots in our sibling experience. How we communicate and especially how we cope with interpersonal conflict all have significant learning arcs as we grow up with siblings.

Probably most powerful of all influences is the effect by siblings on our sense of vulnerability and inadequacy. Our siblings are constant mirrors during our childhood. She gets an "A" in reading, and I am struggling to read and can't stand to do so. I am very musical, and she doesn't seem to be able to carry a tune. We learn about our relative strengths and weaknesses as we watch our siblings grow. We see what gets the attention (and derision) of our parents. Sadness, shame, and feelings of inadequacy are experienced. Exiles are formed. Protective Parts come to the "rescue." Self is constrained. Healing is needed. Exploring sibling stories will inevitably allow for a befriending of deeply buried Exiles. As these feelings are accepted and attended to by the newly liberated Self, the child patient feels unburdened and is even able to extend caring and compassion to a previously conflictual sibling relationship. New dimensions of relating are now possible.

10

WORKING WITH TEENS

Applying IFS Therapy to teens can be very effective. Most adolescents are referred for treatment because of extreme behavior. They are struggling with intense feelings and experiences and tend to cope with these feelings by either applying the "brake" or "accelerator" (Managers and Firefighters) to avoid the pain of these experiences. Parents and teachers clash with these Parts and challenge the teen to change. This challenge creates a Parts-to-Parts interaction that tends to escalate into negative recursive cycles within the family. Instead of resolving matters, parents and teens become locked in battle with one another.

Frank is overwhelmed with school demands and social pressures. He began dabbling with drugs and found that smoking pot relaxed him. While this is a strategy that works to soothe the emotional pain in the short run, avoidance of school work just intensifies the problem, which gets compounded by pressure from parents and school officials to stop avoiding (pot smoking) and start working (school work). The battles that ensue create greater negativity and feeds avoidance maneuvers, which draws more coercion from adults in his life—the creation of a vicious cycle. Often there is a polarization between parental Manager Parts and teen Firefighter Parts.

The conflict pits parental Managers against Frank's Firefighters, Part-to-Part interaction. The parents drag Frank into therapy so that the therapist can force him to stop these self-defeating behaviors. The skilled IFS therapist does not engage in this futile battle. Instead, he begins by listening to Frank and learns that he is making a first-order choice: "I don't like schoolwork, so I am going to avoid it."—stop something that feels aversive. Parents, in turn, apply their own first-order choices: "We do not want him to fail, so we need to take on the role of disciplinarian and force him to do his work." We end up in a battle of wills with each side doing more of the same and resulting in greater alienation.

The IFS therapist, by contrast, does not enter the "game" in the same way. The therapist listens to the teen and listens to the parents (and teachers). The therapist views the pot smoking as an avoidant, self-protective strategy (Functional Hypothesis). Frank acknowledges the use of pot as an anti-anxiety/self-medicating strategy that works up to a point but that creates many more complications for himself. He engages with the parents (begins to calm Managers) and helps them to see that their strategies, while well-intentioned and "logical," are making things worse regarding their goal of improved school work and certainly regarding the quality of the parent-child relationship.

The focus will now shift. It will be important to gradually and safely allow Frank to bring forth feelings of discomfort about his abilities. This is met with Acceptance by the therapist. In family sessions Acceptance of these feelings by the parents is also fostered. Over time, the focus shifts from a problem-saturated conversation to a solution-focused discussion. The shift is now brought to a second-order level where Frank will need to face his anxieties and go *toward* the feelings (Self-energy) and tolerate the struggle inherent in this process. Frank's parents will begin to realize that coercive actions do not solve problems and may compound them.

The IFS therapist will need to realize and appreciate that helping a teen move from an avoidant/Firefighter stance to an approach/Self-directed stance is arduous. Avoidance of pain is built in to the human condition. In addition, the recent generation of parents is prone to protect their kids before they trip and fall, thereby intensifying an already low frustration-tolerance level. Shifting from a first-order strategy to a second-order strategy runs counter to many people's thinking. IFS is a second-order model of intervention that encourages the focus and attention on emotional discomfort, harnessing the Self of the therapist to help remove constraints on the teen and parents, leading them to interact in a Self-to-Self manner.

It has long been held that adolescence is a time of identity definition. Prior to the teen years, the diversity among children is present, but there is little expectation to overtly declare who one is cognitively and emotionally. As they progress in age, teens are expected to take on more responsibility for how they think and feel. The transition from dependency to independence picks up speed. For some this goes well. For others this is scary, with the application of the "brake" and "accelerator," leading to a bumpy ride. This transition reaches an apex with the expected launch to college or work after high school. This launch sometimes goes awry, with the young adult exhibiting extreme psychological symptomatology. Some say that this is a biologically driven process. Others (Haley, 1980) claim that leaving home is fraught with anxiety, leaving the emotional system on overload and creating or contributing to the formation of psychosis and severe depression. In addition, the therapist will need to monitor the impact of peer influence, the "second family" on the day-to-day life of the teen.

Launching from one's family of origin is a powerful point in the family life cycle. Asking the avoidant Parts to step back is a key part of moving this process forward. Therapists need to be extremely patient, respecting the protective nature of such Parts. Why should they trust stepping back? Is it safe to be an unconstrained Self in the context of this family of origin? Once the avoidant Part steps back, what then? No excuses. It will be "just me" out in the world. I will need to take full responsibility for my decisions and actions. The family system may get shaken as homeostasis is threatened. It is inevitable that avoidant Firefighters will be tenacious. The IFS therapist will be tested and likely question the effectiveness of this approach. More than ever, he or she will need to hold fast to the model.

IFS with teens, while full of challenges, can be very rewarding. A very key element in this work is the therapist's ability to remain in Self in the face of stormy behavior. The therapist will be tested by high-intensity Firefighters, including the use of alcohol or drugs, eating disorders, cutting, aggression, promiscuity, and so on. On the other end of the continuum, albeit less dramatic, there are teens who are isolated, withdrawn, and avoidant of peer interaction. They too are struggling with the process of individuation and are at risk for an aborted launch into adulthood. There will be great pressure by parents, schools, and other agencies to apply first-order solutions—medication, hospitalization, residential programs, etc. This can feel like a high-wire act for the therapist. It is essential at these times to remain centered and to harness the courage of Self to sit with a despondent teen and counsel her extremely anxious parents. Decisions regarding interventions are not easy but will be arrived at when there is a critical mass of Self offered by the therapist and fostered between the patient and parents. This is a critical time, as decisions will lead either to healing possibilities that allow for the return to a path of individuation, or possibly lead to setting the stage for a lifetime of limited functioning as a "psychiatric patient." A therapy that leads to Acceptance of turmoil and an appreciation of its protective nature, illogical as that may seem, will lead the patient and parents safely out of the storm.

The therapy will often be a messy, bumpy ride. The teen client will test the therapist, as will the parents. The challenging nature of this work will be amplified when Attachment Injuries run deep. This results in a lack of trust in the enduring nature of relationships. Predictably, anxiety intensifies when initial progress is seen, often leading to a tailspin and a return to the presenting symptomatology. At such points it is crucial for the therapist to care for his or her own inner doubt and anxiety, to remain steady and to stay located in the IFS MetaModel. There will be a gravitational pull toward first-order solutions by the teen and parents as well as for the therapist. The clinician, remaining in Self, will take a crucial leadership position by guiding the treatment on a second-order plane. Gradually, maintaining this position will provide a secure healing location.

It will be essential for the therapist dealing with the extreme Parts of teens to have a supportive peer group available to support and confer with regarding interventions, and, most importantly, staying in Self. The scared, panicky Parts of the therapist will need generous doses of healing Self energy from within and from colleagues.

11

INSIDE THE CHILD'S BODY

Ultimately, the therapist guides the child on an inner journey. The child's feelings are invited into the therapy process. These feelings, or Parts, reside in the child's body. Much of what is experienced as psychological struggle is the relationship that the child has with her feelings. Protective Parts exist to Manage, block, and soothe painful feelings. This drama takes place in the body. It will be very important for the therapist to work somatically. "Where is the fear located?" "When you feel this sadness, what are you aware of going on in your chest . . . in your stomach . . . any other places?" "How do you feel toward this feeling?" Almost always there are feelings (Protective Parts) that fight or want to get rid of such difficult feelings. This is normalized, followed by the therapist asking the child to work with critical or non-accepting Parts. Safely and gradually working toward a full Acceptance of all feelings is encouraged (Functional Hypothesis on somatic level).

The therapist conveys his or her Acceptance and befriends the Protective Parts and the feeling as the client is doing the same. This is the process of Self-attending to the these feelings. Repetition of this sequence is powerfully curative and is a re-programming of the child's system of emotional reactivity.

McConnell (2013) has been an innovator of Somatic IFS Therapy. The essence of her work is to help the client gain access to the bodily manifestations of the emotions. This will be followed by an articulation of these feelings. The client is then directed to bring Self-energy to the various places in the body that are the expressions of Protective Parts (Managers and Firefighters). Ultimately, Self is directed to bring its presence to the emotional pain manifested in somatic form. Self energy is directed to Exiles—befriend it, comfort it, and unburden and free up the body. The therapist and child can use their combined creativity to bring about this healing process.

Children who internalize will likely find this process easier to learn than children who habitually externalize their complaints. The therapist can guide externalizers by going first outside, then inside their bodies.

The child can be asked to watch a "movie" where he (or a child character) is on the screen. "What are you thinking?" "What are you feeling?" "Where in your body is the feeling located?" Much patience needs to be harnessed for this process, but the therapeutic payoff can be powerful. Many kids respond to drawing their feelings or characters that have certain feelings. They are encouraged to talk about this. Some nonverbal kids can be encouraged to "play out" their feelings on toy drums or other percussive instruments.

Therapists will do well to watch for incongruity or metacommunication, i.e., when the child says "I'm fine" but her facial expressions conveys "I'm worried." It is my belief that these incongruities take a toll on the body, in children as well as in parents, leading to body tension, elevated blood pressure, etc. With a gentle approach, observing and asking about the incongruity can be powerfully healing. If parents and children try to override their feelings, unwilling to accept that there are limits to their control of certain situations emotionally and physically, the body will react with aspects of hyper- or hypo-arousal (this will be further discussed in the section on Twelve-Step Programs). Over time, this can have a permanent and damaging impact on the body.

The Sensorimotor Therapy Model (Ogden, Minton & Pain, 2006) teaches that with kids (and many adults), effective therapy can happen in a top-down treatment process (talking/thinking providing access to feelings) as well as bottom-up treatment process (feelings providing access to talking/thinking). The greater the therapist's flexibility, the wider range of children the healing process will reach.

The therapist can introduce breathing and relaxation exercises to the child. These exercises can create a safe way to gain access to feelings and ultimately to speak directly to them with the therapist's guidance. Over time, the child can learn to do this internal comforting on their own.

Sandy, a ten year-old girl, told me that she was very angry at her friend Tammy for not including her in a weekend get together. I asked her to plant her feet firmly on the floor and follow my lead in breathing in through her nose, holding the breath for a moment, then releasing the breath through her mouth. After several repetitions I asked Sandy where the anger is located in her body. She said that her chest feels very tight. When asked how she feels toward this feeling, she said that she hates it and wants to get rid of it. I asked her if the Part that hates the anger can step back a bit so we can talk directly to the anger. She seemed to "get" this and said OK. Next, I directed Sandy to send some breath to the tightness in her chest so that the angry feelings can feel her presence. She did so and said she was feeling a little more relaxed. I asked her if she new what she was feeling a few seconds before the anger/tension entered her body. "Sad" she said, at not being included with friends. I asked her where she feels the sadness. She said that it is in her stomach, like a queasy feeling.

I asked how she feels toward the queasiness and she said she felt sorry for it. I again directed her to send some breath to the feeling in her stomach. "How does the queasiness feel now?" Starting to relax. . . . This led to a discussion about other situations where she has felt left out and a beginning of our addressing how to comfort herself at such times and what she may want to say to her friends. Therapists are directed to my forthcoming (2014) therapeutic board game, *Kids World: Inside and Out* for a fun, child-friendly way to access their thoughts and feelings including many IFS and mindfulness exercises that help the child identify and work through challenging life experiences.

The healing process will ultimately include the body's realignment and centering—another way of manifesting Self-leadership. Over time, the therapist can check in with the child and revisit the bodily manifestations of the feelings: "How is that tension in your chest doing?" "When you were taking the social studies test, did you feel that fluttering in your stomach? If so, more or less than usual? How were you able to help it?" "Were you aware of those critical Parts? How did you respond to those Parts?," and so on. In this way, I believe, neurobiological responses become re-programmed. Here and at any time the therapist is performing an "ecological check," as a way to call upon and track the internal emotional system of the child. This will provide valuable feedback for continuing therapeutic work.

Speaking from Self

As Manager and Firefighter Protective Parts are encountered, and, as these Parts can unblend from Self, the therapist can coach the family members to represent powerful feelings felt in the body. Instead of being embedded as Managers and Firefighters and instead of the raw flooding of Exiles (intense sadness, fear, feelings of inadequacy, shame), with the help of the calmness, clarity, and courage of Self, these feelings can be conveyed between and among parents and children. Now that the survival agendas have been separated from Self, important emotive experiences can be stated more effectively and received in a way that is more likely to bring a compassionate empathic response. This is the result of intrapsychic and relational healing, and this ongoing process will serve to maintain the important gains and spur continued emotional growth. So, instead of a teen-parent battle about doing chores or schoolwork, the teen can speak about his worries and represent his hurt feelings to his parents. Likewise, the parents can be coached to shift from a coercive/Managerial mode of communication to being able to express their good intentions in protecting their youngster.

Parents can be coached to talk about their worries and perhaps feelings that have been triggered from their own history. Gradually, the

Part-to-Part battle will transform to a Self-to-Self connection so that feelings will be validated, comforting will ensue, and secure Attachment will be fostered.

Speaking from Self will represent congruency in what is being felt in the body and what is being communicated interpersonally. Disparate metacommunications will diminish. Verbal and nonverbal communication will be consonant. As this gradually becomes the dominant mode of experience, the child will feel more free in his or her breathing and bodily tensions will lift. It will be so very important for the therapist to monitor this with the child so that this healthy experience can be "captured" and anchored for future reference.

Part Three

BEYOND THE FAMILY

12

THE CHILD IN LARGER CONTEXTS

The MetaModel and Schools

IFS therapy with kids and their families will very often require coordination and work with key school personnel—teachers, principals, school counselors, psychologists, and social workers. From the point of view of the school, responding to any individual child's behavior will have to be done in the larger context of maintaining stability, peace, and decorum in the classroom and extended school environment. While the IFS therapist may have the "luxury" of sitting patiently with the agitated child, the school can tolerate this only up to the point where teachers' and other students' safety and unobstructed learning environment are at risk.

By definition, then, school systems will have to be more conservative in allowance of disordered behavior than will the therapist. The IFS therapist will need to acknowledge this situation and carefully and respectfully take this into account. It is very important for the therapist to cultivate ongoing relationships with school personnel. Being readily available for crisis calls is a must, as are frequent check-ins and school meetings to track the progress of the interventions. Trust between the school and therapist will help everyone to weather difficult situations.

It will be important for the therapist to introduce the school personnel to the thinking of the IFS MetaModel. For the most part, I have found high receptivity to this thinking and have seen growing confidence in the model as they experience me being totally available to work along with them, especially with high-risk cases.

While I am very sensitized to melding my approach with the needs and constraints of the school environment, I do take an assertive stance as an advocate of my child and teen patients. I often try to slow down the tendency of schools to label and classify students, referring kids for medication and placing them in remedial programs. I convey the need to consider such interventions, but also have schools consider the psychological fallout for a child carrying a label. As kindly and well intentioned as schools can be, children often feel pathologized by this "helping" process. So, these attempts at immediate solutions can lead in the long run to children who feel deficient and inadequate throughout their developing years.

The best way to defuse this situation is to include child and parents fully in the decision-making process. Talking about the pros and cons of special education and/or medication and allowing time for making determinations is essential. Inviting children to diagnostic and planning meetings conveys respect for the child's feelings and input toward choices and directions. This process needs to continue over time. Within this structure parents and children will not feel coerced or invalidated. Being included in all discussions and decision-making is a collaborative and respectful process. While time consuming, the results will be much more of a "team effort" for the education process, diminishing oppositional tendencies that ultimately will defeat even the best of interventions.

This process will be decision-making from a Self-led position. Trust in the process will grow and the child and parents will experience the school system as an ally to their family system. Rather than feeling defeated, shamed, and inadequate, working in this way will bring compassion to the family-school relationship, clarity to the issues at hand, and will foster confidence in the youngster. The school will have a student who fully participates in all aspects of his or her course of education.

Treatment of Families Within Our Culturally Diverse Society

The most fundamental underlying premise of family systems thinking is that problems and symptoms can be understood by taking into account the multiple contexts in which they are embedded. Everything else flows from this base. As we have discussed, psychological struggles both mild and severe will be seen as adaptive and survival based when the child's emotional system is viewed as interactive and coping with the interpersonal world around her. We have looked at the context of family and school. It will be very crucial for therapists to also bring the larger culture into the treatment room. Beliefs, rituals, and traditions all impact children and their parents. It behooves each therapist to be highly sensitive and mindful of this broader circle in which the child and family live (McGoldrick, Pearce & Giordano, 1982).

It can be stated, with the possible exception of Native Americans, that all families in America have a history and legacy of immigrant origins. Some came to this country of their own free will and others, notably African Americans and oppressed refugees fleeing for their lives, came here against their will or as a matter of basic survival. While cultures influence expectations of child development, it is the author's opinion that the "job description" of parents of all cultures is the same: to foster physical and emotional health, safety, and security in their children and to guide each child toward maturity and a sense of competence and self-efficacy. This is akin to a child's bill of rights.

Practices that interfere with these universal human rights occur in some families. Violation of the physical or emotional integrity of the person, such as physical or sexual abuse and marital violence can never be excused, regardless of cultural background. More subtle practices such as coercive male privilege are equally destructive. Thus, there are two significant ground rules when considering cultural influences. First, therapeutic interventions, to be effective, must be applied with a careful understanding of cultural context. Second, any practices that diminish the status of an individual within a family system and serve to oppress another human being cannot be excused as culture-bound and must be sensitively but emphatically challenged by the therapist.

On a societal scale, oppression in the form of discrimination against minority cultures and policies that foster poverty lead to a sense of powerlessness for families. This will block the development and opportunity for self-efficacy, thereby disqualifying the child's journey towards individuation. This experience will prime such children for oppositionalism in their families, schools, and neighborhoods.

The recent emphasis on achievement testing in the schools is aimed at measuring outcomes. Attempts to teach strategies that raise these scores are another first-order solution. My hope is that educators and politicians will be mindful of the need to provide resources for impoverished families so that each child is embedded in a safe, secure, and growth-promoting environment. This is a second-order solution and will deliver durable results, that is, higher scores achieved by more secure and hopeful kids. At an early point in my career, I was called upon to serve as consultant to a Head Start Program in a neighboring community, consisting mostly of minority, low-income, single-parent families. This was a wonderful early education program. In addition to a soft, gentle approach to the kids and reliable availability to the parents, we arranged for Pizza Wednesdays—providing a meal for the kids, siblings, and parents after the school day each week. We ate, talked, and laughed together. Bonds of trust were cultivated. A loving community fostered a secure base from which kids could learn and families felt safe. This simple structure represents school-as-community at its best. Just as Self energy is applied to the healing of Exiles, the Self energy contained in school systems has much healing potential to help raise up parents and youngsters who feel "less than" others, a feeling that erodes their chances of growing into success.

Clinicians working with families will need to be cognizant of the variety of beliefs and customs of many cultures by spending time and listening closely to each family's story. Clinicians will need to serve as strong advocates for empowering families and ensuring that equality and respect are the rules that govern family life.

97

The Family Doctor

When I was growing up in the 1950s we had a family doctor. He treated my parents, my older brother, and me. His office was across the street from our building, and most of the time if we were not feeling well we would cross the street and be seen in the office. If we ran a fever, even during the night, my parents would call and the doctor would make a house call. We had a relationship with this doctor until we left home to make our way in the world. I remember that my mother would speak to the doctor about our physical health and also ask for advice regarding our behavior and developmental milestones. It was a comfort to have this professional "on call" to our family throughout our childhood and adolescence.

The pioneers of family therapy tended to model a short-term treatment for children and families. I was supervised by Jay Haley, who advocated a problem-solving approach that centered on a powerful intervention that would aim at resolving the presenting problem in a thorough, systemic manner. Haley's belief was that this intervention would change the choreography of the family, so that following the brief treatment family members would be able to handle future issues in healthier ways on their own.

While my interventions are still systems-based, diagnosing and changing not only the problem but also the family members' relationship to the problems, I have come to believe that a quick exit by the therapist is not always the wisest choice. For families, life happens: children grow, siblings are born, relatives die, illnesses occur, and the family configuration often changes in our modern world. There is diminishing support from relatives and extended family these days, and for the most part medical practitioners are no longer working in a way that allows them to provide more than a 15-minute office visit for the immediate illness. The family life cycle is an ongoing saga of gains and losses. Even more complicated than this, sometimes a gain can feel like a psychological loss for some families, particularly when attachment injuries continue their powerful grip, as when a child is launched to college or gets married. Sometimes a gain for one family member is a loss for another, as when a parent gets remarried and a child mourns the loss of the family structure as he has known it.

So, just like my family doctor from my childhood, I believe that there is a great value to remain available to a family as they navigate the curves of life and need guidance regarding how much to put their foot on the brake and how much on the accelerator. When the initial referral problem is sufficiently resolved or adapted to, parents will often ask for extended work on their marital interaction. Sometimes additional work with a sibling will be desired. At times the original identified child patient herself will ask to come in for periodic sessions, perhaps monthly or even every few months for a check-in. This "family doctor" approach has been particularly useful in guiding families through divorce and remarriage and helping kids who struggle with learning issues throughout their school years. The ripple effects of these events and issues take on different forms, cognitively and emotionally, at different life stages. For example, I have worked extensively with many youngsters on the autism spectrum along with their parents and siblings, who have benefited from such long-term care. Dealing with the struggles of emotional intelligence in elementary school are quite different than the struggles when graduating from high school and seeking employment and possible independent living arrangements. I do not impose this belief on my clients. Instead, I listen carefully and discuss their needs frequently. The treatment plan is always up for revision. I feel honored to have guided scores of families in this manner over the years.

Part Four

CHALLENGING ASPECTS OF THERAPY WITH CHILDREN, TEENS, AND THEIR FAMILIES

13

FREQUENTLY ASKED QUESTIONS IN WORKING WITH THE INTERNAL FAMILY SYSTEMS METAMODEL

How useful is DSM-V?

The Diagnostic and Statistical Manual is a nosological system that lists the plethora of symptoms and personality disorders manifested by human beings. It is a medical model compendium compiled mostly by psychiatrists. DSM-V is a list of illnesses that need to be cured. This, again, is a pathology-oriented approach to the patient. There are very few "conditions" that relate to a systems view (rare examples are oppositional disorder of childhood and post-traumatic stress disorder—these syndromes cannot exist in a vacuum). This list is a nominalization, that is, it turns a process into a condition, thereby rendering it an "illness." An example is turning "sadness" into "depression," and without much effort viewing this human process as an illness possibly requiring medication without accounting for its normative features when viewed within multiple contexts.

Because this is an official list, mental health professionals begin to believe its independent "truth"; in turn, insurance carriers determine that these conditions meet the requirement of "medical necessity" for treatment; patients have no other recourse but to accept and resign themselves to their "illness."

A much more relational and context-oriented diagnostic description is needed. Some attempts at this have been made. The politics of the healthcare hierarchy will be hard to budge in altering this structure. It will be important for progressively oriented clinicians to recognize and assert the dangers of this diagnostic system.

What Is Resistance?

In many therapy models, patients who have difficulty with change or begin to change and then become stuck again in unproductive symptom patterns are labeled "resistant." Extremely difficult patients are often given the more severe diagnostic labels such as "borderline," personality disorder, etc.

From a systems point of view, embedded in an adaptational belief system, resistance to change is absolutely normal. If symptoms are attempts at survival, isn't it natural that it would be very difficult to give them up and try new psychological strategies? In addition, the family system has an ecology all its own and will need to adjust to the changing of any of its Parts. Very likely, the family will need to be addressed in order to adapt to the changing client. A course of therapy without ups and downs and without "resistance," is most likely an incomplete treatment, or a treatment that has stayed mostly on the surface of the client's complaints.

Resistance is normal. Milton Erickson once said to me that resistance means that the therapist lacks a flexible and wide-ranging approach to treatment. If we are trained in only one model, then a percentage of our clients will never get better. The successful therapist will be one who is able to shift styles and strategies in accordance with the needs of clients for comprehensive treatment. Careful listening without preconceived "answers," adopting the "beginner's mind" of the Zen master, and engaging in a respectful conversation with the client will most often draw forth the natural healing process in human beings.

The evolving field of strategic therapy documents the most long-standing and creative commitment to the notion of resistance and change. The successful therapist will need to pull up the strategy needed at a given time, much like a computer user will call upon multiple "windows" in order to complete a task.

Is There a Typical Trajectory of Change in the Process of Psychotherapy?

While each case will differ in specific characteristics, the process of change will usually proceed as follows: After establishing an effective therapeutic alliance, especially one in which symptoms are embraced and recognized for their adaptive purposes, it is typical that these defensive/self-protective aspects of the person will diminish and hopefulness will ensue. This may be followed by a period of stability, which will often get interrupted by environmental events triggering emotional responses that once again call forth the overworked survival patterns. Symptoms will return or perhaps intensify. The client will typically feel defeated. Very often, the therapist will also feel thwarted. It is critical that at these times the therapist can guide the client and "normalize" this dip in progress.

It can be very useful for therapists to prepare clients for this likelihood earlier in the sequence so that both will be prepared for this event. This would diminish the likelihood of therapy dropouts. Many therapists neglect to keep this very normal sequence of events in mind.

As the therapist guides the client through this difficult experience, which can be brief or prolonged, much additional learning can occur, leading to more extensive change in the intrapsychic and/or relational system of the client. It should be noted that there may be many such waves of improvement followed by struggles (old and new) during a course of therapy.

Attention needs to be paid to the presence of Attachment Injuries held as Exiles for children and their parents. As discussed earlier in this book, this psychic pain will powerfully color the degree of safety that the client will feel about emotional change. Ultimately I believe that for the vast majority of cases self-sustaining change occurs when significant unburdening of intrapsychic pain is accomplished.

What is the Nature of Confidentiality in the Practice of Family Therapy?

Questions about confidentiality are among the most frequently asked by practitioners, especially early on in their training or when initially exposed to systems thinking and treatment. Traditionally, confidentiality is handled in a "boilerplate" manner by most clinicians. Unless information revealed in treatment is deemed to be dangerous and life threatening to either the patient, some person in the patient's life, or both, information is guarded and protected within the therapeutic relationship. This, of course, is one of the curative factors of psychotherapy—another human being can be trusted to listen to just about anything in a safe and non-judgmental manner.

Family therapists would agree with the power and healing nature of protection of information. However, from a systems perspective, confidentiality also means boundaries and privacy and is not a purely all-or-none issue. The issue of proximity-distance is one of the prime dimensions around which psychological symptomatology is formed. It is around this dimension that the Structural Family Therapy Model of Salvador Minuchin, MD, revolves. At times, a family may have very loose boundaries in relationships. This enmeshed family type would tend to have unclear boundaries and hierarchy, negate differences, diminish or avoid conflict, and produce children with low frustration tolerance and high dependency needs. At the other end of the spectrum is the disengaged family with too rigid boundaries and compartmentalization among members and subgroups. This family system would tend to emphasize differences and self-reliance and would tend to have children with tenuous bonding to parents and other adults. Often, children in these families are defiant, aggressive, and antisocial. Both extremes of the spectrum represent polarized forms of insecure Attachment. The psychologically healthy family would fall somewhere in the middle of this continuum, having semi-permeable barriers of communication, sometimes being open, at other times respecting privacy. This family would be able to adapt well to the challenges of life.

In accordance with the above model, confidentiality in families is a process and experience, not simply a point of assurance that can be offered by a therapist. Families need to find their level and climate of comfort with issues like parent-child boundaries.

Also, these boundaries need to be adjusted as children grow into adolescence and adulthood. In therapy, the clinician needs to help the family grapple with the emotional repercussions of the proximity-distance dimension. In other words, families, with the therapist's help, need to "sweat out" the struggle of healthy boundaries at various points along the life cycle. Thus, confidentiality cannot be simply a pat guarantee made by the therapist. The need for privacy and sharing and the impact on each family member is a crucial aspect of the process of family and marital therapy. It is now known that when trauma is accompanied by secrecy and shame, the long term psychological dysfunction will be much greater than had the person been able to express and process the emotional impact at the time of the trauma (Courtois, 1988; Herman, 1992). A balance between self-disclosure and privacy is a hallmark of the healthy family.

How Do the Space and Time Dimensions Impact the Family Life Cycle?

Family members, by definition, are existentially linked to one another. You can quit your job or end a friendship but you are "stuck" with your family. You cannot not be a son, a daughter, a father, a mother, or a sibling. We are all born into these roles and live within their confines throughout our lifetimes. This "no-escape" clause of life leads to a set of constraints. However, we do discover early on that there are also degrees of freedom within the borders of our existentially prescribed roles.

The degrees of freedom are in the space and time dimensions. As mentioned above, we discover that we can change and control the degree of closeness and distance to our family members. We also discover that this is a basic psychological survival mechanism.

Most symptoms can be seen to have a spatial aspect. Oppositional children are able to keep parents involved in their lives while at the same time pushing them away. Anxiety often leads to fight (approaching the feared situation) or flight (avoiding the feared situation). Depression will lead to social withdrawal, with others reacting pro or con. The fantasies of psychosis will create a safer "reality" to retreat to for a patient struggling with intense psychic pain. Dissociation is a symptom that employs space (and time) in order to distance from trauma and terror.

In addition to the spatial dimension, time is also a degree of freedom that can be manipulated by our minds. For instance, an adolescent or adult can behave in a childlike manner. A child can take on a parental or adult level of responsibility. Transitions in the progression of the family life cycle are key elements in the time dimension. Jay Haley, Betty Carter, Monica McGoldrick and other pioneers of our field have recognized that symptom formation is inextricably linked to change over time experienced by the family in its life cycle.

Symptoms are more likely to occur at or around significant life transitions—entrance to school, beginning of adolescence, launching to college, illness or death of a grandparent, etc. In addition, "normal" and inevitable life transitions can be tinged with intergenerational anxiety and sadness. The birth of a new baby, usually viewed as a joyous event in the life of a family may be experienced as a "loss" by a grandparent who needs to hold their offspring (now a parent) in a childlike position; a child's adolescence will be fraught with anxiety for a parent who had experimented with psychedelic drugs themselves during this corresponding developmental stage.

So in the existentially "given" progression of life, growth from an infant through childhood to adolescence, adulthood, marriage, midlife, and older years to death will likely be complicated by significant emotional overlay at some points along the way.

The successful family learns to negotiate the inevitable changes along the way, applying the emotional "brake" or "accelerator" as needed. Too much or too little intervention on the time dimension will create a pressure on the natural growth processes of the family system and result in symptom formation.

How Frequent Should Therapy Sessions Be? How Long Does it Take for a Successful Course of Treatment?

The discussion of frequency of sessions and length of treatment comes mainly from the psychoanalytic literature. Traditional psychoanalysis posits that a thorough course of treatment would require several sessions per week over a several-year span of time. Anything less than this would be seen as incomplete treatment, perhaps prematurely terminated by the "resistant" or "acting-out" patient without the sanction of the analyst.

Once again, this view represents an orthodoxy and assumption that the therapist and/or the model represent the standard or "truth" that all patients need to comply with.

In my experience over the past several decades, I have found that most individuals, couples, and families use therapy very effectively attending one session per week (45 minutes to 1 hour, depending on the therapist's style and the clients' needs) for 1–2 years. It can be very helpful for clients to digest and metabolize the learning from each session in the intervening week. In addition, a weekly interval conveys respect and support of the survival skills and real life responsibilities of the client.

There certainly are times when more than one session per week and/or additional telephone contact is greatly helpful. This is particularly the case when a current crisis needs more attention and guidance. How does one determine when to structure the treatment in this manner? Ask your clients and discuss their needs.

While termination from therapy is treated in the psychoanalytic literature as a long-term standard process, reality shows that each person or family terminates in their own way, sometimes in a neat and tidy manner with a gradual taper before finishing, sometimes in a more abrupt manner, announcing that they are satisfied with the results and stating that they need some time on their own to consolidate the gains made.

At times clients will say that at a given time they have come as far as they can for now and recognize that more work may be done at a later point. My view is that a family therapist does well to be a true "family practitioner," that is, a mental health guide or coach who is available to the family members throughout their life cycle. For example, a couple who are in therapy for marital issues may call at a later point in order to deal with the stresses of child-focused problems, concerns about a frail grandparent, etc. The greater the range of skills and knowledge held by the therapist, the more effective he or she will be in treating the widest range of presenting problems. One sure aspect of reality is that over time, life continues to happen. Having a skilled therapist to call upon is like having a special ally to accompany you on this journey.

It would be wonderful if the mental health professional was more widely recognized as a resource to be called upon throughout the family life cycle. The main emphasis here is that the therapy process should be a collaborative venture and not a set process dictated by the therapist's belief system.

Dealing with Anger

Among the most difficult sessions are those where anger is the dominant emotion. Child versus parent. Sibling battles. Parent against parent, client against therapist. Human nature is such that there are two directions for relationships saturated with anger. Anger of one person will beget anger from their counterpart or, on the other hand, anger in one person will trigger withdrawal in the other. Both of these outcomes represent protective strategies and are part of human evolutionary nature. Such interactions will be unproductive and feel defeating to the family. The therapist will feel defeated as well, often becoming combative or withdrawn. These sessions tend to ruin the therapist's day.

The therapist's first step is to address the anger and attempt disarmament. Viewing anger as a "signal" that there is a threat to deal with is useful. Beyond this, anger will interfere with the building of mutual understanding between the dyad and lead to escalation and prolonged warfare.

It is useful to view anger as a Part of the person, but not the center or compassionate Self of the person. The client will feel relieved to have the anger addressed as a Part and not the person him or herself.

The next step is to disengage the dyad from the dominance of anger. It can be helpful to talk with them about appreciating anger as a "signal." Then, the therapist appeals to each person or to the angry Part itself (help clients locate the part physically within their bodies). Ask the angry Part to step back in order to create some space for new work or new understandings to emerge. Most often this is possible. The angry Part is not seeking destruction; it is a self-protective force. Often, Exiles are just below the explosion. If the therapist can construct sufficient safety in the session, the anger will recede, at least for some of the session. It can be useful to ask clients to articulate what the "subtitles" on the screen might be when anger erupts, i.e., "what is underneath the anger?" Also, trying to capture what the client was feeling in the moments prior to anger erupting will also point the trail to the Exiles of hurt, sadness, and feelings of inadequacy.

There are occasions when the anger, driven by an intense sense of fear and threat, will not easily retreat. When this occurs, the therapist can "surrender" to the anger of the moment by stating that the dyad will need to use this session to be on the attack. The therapist can normalize that all families reach this point at times. The individuals should be told that while the anger is dominant, they should not expect anything productive to come of their discussion and that the therapy will not be helpful under these circumstances. They can be given an option to end the session early or to stay while fighting unproductively. This process of "surrender" on the part of the therapist can, at times, serve to jumpstart a more productive discussion; sometimes not.

At times virulent anger is compounded with a sense of shame. Each family member may be beyond the point of safety to show their vulnerable side with the other partner in close proximity—showing "weakness" in the midst of a battle is not a good strategy as is experienced by each individual. It can be useful at such times to separate the dyad and to work with one person at a time. This separation can help to defuse the volatility. Under such circumstances, many individuals will be able to reach a calmer internal state. It may be possible to resume work as a dyad in this or subsequent sessions, or it may be more helpful to have a series of individual sessions with each partner before coming together again in a joint session.

It is essential, as it is a challenge, for the child and family therapist to stay centered in the heat of the anger and blame. The therapist will need to develop internal strategies in order to stay on track.

Nurturing from Self to "battered" Parts of the therapist is essential at quiet moments of the workday. It is critical for the therapist to exercise self-care when his or her Parts have been activated. Keeping the promise to one's Self is essential for repairing the impact of the client's assault.

How Helpful Is Giving Advice to Families?

On the surface, giving direct advice is what many families may expect from the therapist, an expert in the field of mental health and emotional well-being. However, families will respond to advice in a multitude of ways, sometimes puzzling the therapist and sometimes, when not following the guidance, leading the therapist to conclude that these are "resistant" clients. It is hoped that the following discussion will help to clarify this process.

As explicated in many parts of this book, according to the Mental Research Institute in Palo Alto (Watzlawick et al., 1974; Fraser & Solovey, 2007) there are two types of therapeutic change. First-order change takes place in a linear, concrete, straightforward manner. The individual, couple, or family will ask the therapist a question, he or she will make a suggestion, they will follow his or her directions and report back as to the success of the advice. If necessary, the therapist will fine-tune the suggestion until it meets the desired outcome for the clients. The therapy remains problem-to-solution focused. In my experience, First-order change works fully with a small percentage of client families, or works only partially with another small percentage. The reasons for this are varied. I believe that families and couples who are at the early stages of their relationships are more malleable and thus more receptive to direct advice. There has been less time for defensive build-up and for rigidification and toxicity around certain issues. In child-focused cases, children will respond to concrete suggestions and reinforcers (rewards, behavioral charts, etc.) early in life, while the same interventions will fall flat several years later in development. Part of this is development of greater degrees of abstract thinking (Piaget, 1962) and also the "stuckness" or rigidity of patterns that evolve in family systems. As strategies of adaptation (Functional Hypothesis) are repeated and over-employed, they become automatic responses felt to be necessary for emotional survival and not easily relinquished. Interestingly, in books and articles on behavioral (first-order) techniques there is often mention in the preface (or in a footnote) that the success of these techniques tends to peak at age eight with a sharp decline as the child is older, supporting some of the above observations regarding children and families.

In addition, as discussed throughout this book, the history of Attachment Injury compounds the problems at hand. The giving of advice is greatly complicated by the emotional context of lack of trust and

110

dependability in others. In fact, along with the factors mentioned here, the degree to which there is avoidance or noncompliance with direct advice serves as a diagnostic sign regarding the presence of deep-seated Attachment Injuries.

The Palo Alto group next mentions second-order change, change that takes place as a result of a shift in the context or system in which the problem is embedded. This is a much more frequent scenario. In order for a child-focused problem to change, reactions to the child by parents often need adjustment, siblings' feelings may need to be accounted for, and work with teachers and other school personnel may be necessary, in addition to a shift intrapsychically for the youngster attending to emotional pain. The impact of the change on the family as a whole will need to be considered. For most families, the therapist will be dealing with lifelong thoughts, beliefs, behaviors, and feelings that have served defensive and protective purposes (Functional Hypothesis), but which actually backfire when over-employed. In traditional diagnostic schemas, these patterns are called "personality disorders." Noncompliance or "resistance" will be the norm in most courses of therapy. The therapist should expect this and, therefore, expect that giving advice will likely not be fully effective. There is no harm to try to give homework assignments, suggestions, etc. The clients' responses (or lack thereof) will be very revealing. Sometimes initial compliance will slide back into old patterns. The therapist should not get discouraged by this common process. It just means that larger-scale systems shifts will be needed. Special attention to the Attachment capabilities and constraints of our clients is essential in this regard.

How Helpful Are Twelve-Step Programs in Work with Children and Their Families?

Many people have been helped through participation in Twelve-Step Programs. Originating as Alcoholics Anonymous, these programs address all kinds of "addictions"—alcoholism, substance abuse, gambling, overeating, excessive spending, promiscuity, etc. What do all of these behaviors have in common? Essentially, these are Parts of our personalities that function as elements of soothing and stimulation. These aspects of our makeup serve to directly relieve stress and keep us from becoming overwhelmed by feelings of loss, sadness, and fear. The addictions protect us against our vulnerability as human beings. They provide a "quick fix" or serve as emotional Firefighters that lessen our discomfort.

People who make excessive use of these quick-fix mechanisms ("addictions") seem to be in an intense internal battle against the experience of vulnerability. They feel better in the short run by reaching for a drink, taking a drug, gambling large sums of money, overeating, engaging in promiscuity, and so on. However, in the long run, these "solutions" create very serious new problems, among which are compromising health even to the point of death, wreaking havoc on family life, existing in a cognitively altered state, losing jobs, accruing major debt, etc. It seems that the greater the exiled feelings of sadness and fear, the greater the investment some people have in blotting out the surfacing of such emotions.

Some claim that the addictions have a genetic component. Indeed, these patterns do seem to run in families. One could debate how much environment conditions the body or how much biology impacts behavior. I believe that there probably exist recursive loops of feedback from both components.

Twelve-Step Programs allow the addicted person to accept his or her vulnerable side in an atmosphere of support and fellowship, structured through meetings and peer sponsors.

The essential credo of this organization is the following Serenity Prayer (Niebhur, circa 1937, as included in *The Big Book*, 2001): "(God) grant me the serenity to accept the things I cannot change, courage to change the things I can, and wisdom to know the difference." In one terse statement, a guide and belief system is set up that allows the person to give up the fight, accept the "disease" (alcoholism, gambling, etc.), and thereby yield to one's human frailties. This organization's reframing of the problem is tremendously powerful. The individual actually surrenders to his or her inevitable vulnerabilities. Surrounding this surrender is a potent support structure: Twelve-Step program meetings are located in many convenient locations at all times of day, night, and weekends; if one travels out of town or abroad, meetings are available; peer sponsors are on call 24 hours per day. So, while on the one hand participants yield to their vulnerabilities, on the other hand they are given membership to a community of support that is tremendously protective and safe, and that asks only for sobriety and self-admission that one has a problem over which he or she lacks ultimate power—the addiction.

The Twelve-Step approach is much more powerful than an individual therapist in that it offers round-the-clock support for no fee. In a sense, it provides the "unconditional Acceptance" of ideal parents—and in this sense, it is very curative. Is it compatible or at odds with family therapy? I'd say compatible in the hands of an open-minded, accepting therapist. A systems approach, as mentioned many times in this book, has at its center the belief in the Functional Hypothesis, i.e., the important protective purpose served by the symptom. In this, systems theory is very congruent with Twelve-Step participants. If not stated overtly, the Twelve-Step approach recognizes the survival-based aspects of the addiction.

In addition, the structure of the programs offer curative alternatives, i.e., support and protection without the use of the addiction. Also, Twelve-Step programs build in support groups for family members, such as Adult Children of Alcoholics, Alanon and Gamanon for spouses of alcoholics and compulsive gamblers, Alateen as a support group for teens with parents struggling with addictive behaviors.

It has been my experience that family therapy and Twelve-Step programs can effectively complement one another. As the person becomes abstinent, emotional struggles can be examined from intrapsychic, interpersonal, and intergenerational perspectives.

Very often, a struggle with addictions represents an intense internal polarization between Parts. Most likely this plays out when a Firefighter ("Just take another drink. Who cares?") is countered by a Manager ("Don't you dare have another drink. This stuff is killing you."), An intrapsychic battle ensues. Sometimes the Firefighter wins; sometimes the Manager wins. The IFS therapist will recognize this as a dominant, often blended Parts struggle. It can be very helpful to bring these polarized parts together (an internal "Town Meeting," as developed by Ralph Cohen, PhD, personal communication). The purpose of this therapeutic meeting is to bring Self-leadership to each Part and to the conflict. This can be very effective to exit the no-win seesaw battle that creates a stranglehold for the person and his or her relationships. This ultimately moves the discussion from the level of first-order change to second-order change, which engages the client (and family) in an exploration of relationships with the symptom and can lead to the unburdening of Exiles (Fraser & Solvey, 2007).

Some conflict can occur philosophically. Is alcoholism an actual "disease"? Is it absolutely prohibitive for the person to have a drink at a social gathering? If the systems therapist can guide the person and family system through these struggles (just more intense versions of what all of us deal with) and emotionally process such "choices" (a term not liked by Twelve-Step advocates, who hold to absolutes when it comes to problem addictions)—including the choice to even examine this conflict—he or she will be in helpful, therapeutic territory. Helping families deal with addiction, slips from sobriety, new relationships that arise from a newly sober family member, etc. are essential skills for a family systems therapist. It will be very important for the therapist to look at his or her beliefs and to creatively apply these to each such family treated.

Many teen cases circle around the vicious cycle of polarization with addictions (Firefighters). Often they are trying to "drown" the experience of their vulnerability (Exiles). Being able to embrace the wisdom of the Serenity Prayer, in other words, knowing what they are and are not able to be in control of, and to experience this in their bodies can create a reversal: Acceptance of their vulnerability that leads to Self-leadership, which can unburden emotional pain.

Should Children Be Medicated?

Throughout this book, the IFS MetaModel has been presented as a powerful alternative to the Medical Model approach to treatment. The Medical Model is based on prescription of medication and is designed to relieve and diminish symptoms—to lower anxiety, reduce depression, improve attentional capacity, and so on. It is a first-order intervention that works, as do all other treatments, on a continuum from greatly effective, to moderately effective, to having no impact and even to worsening symptoms.

Prescribing medication needs to be considered very carefully as this has many consequences, some of which are overt and some of which remain hidden. There are almost always physiological side effects, short term and long term as psychotropics hit a target that includes areas of the brain and body that are separate from the intended bullseye symptom. On an emotional plane, prescribing medication can define the child as ill, impaired, and unable to have an impact on his or her inner life. It also can place parents in a position of resignation regarding their troubled youngster. At its psychological worst, the medication choice can define a youngster as a chronic "psychiatric patient." This definition can create and/or feed into already existing Exiles and can impair the sense of self-efficacy so powerfully needed for growth into a free, competent, and confident person actualizing their potential. I have treated many adults who gain access to Exiles of anxiety, sadness, and inadequacy regarding decisions made regarding medication in their childhood.

Having stated the above, as noted, sometimes medication can be greatly effective. At times, the parents are very eager and set regarding this choice of treatment. Not infrequently, we are referred a child who is already taking medication. From a clinically potent point of view, then, we need to be flexible and to view medication as part of the "system" that we are dealing with. I usually prefer to counsel parents and kids on trying psychotherapy for several weeks in order to see what type of change we can accomplish before trying medication. If we agree that it might be worth beginning a trial of medication, the decision-making process should be a gradual one with discussions including parents, child, and family together. Arriving at clarity and viewing the use of medication to be of help is important for all concerned and will land in Self-led territory. Once this decision is Self-led on the part of parents and child, the emotional damage will be averted and the use of medication can be viewed in the context of compassion and caring for the Exiled Parts of the youngster. This will then contribute to effective second-order healing. It will be important to frequently return to the issue of medication to make sure that Self remains in leadership regarding this aspect of treatment.

It should be noted that many first-order interventions, like referral for residential treatment facility, special education placement, and so on should likewise be handled in a therapy that is conducted in a collaborative and compassionate manner. The overarching rule? Is the intervention guided by Self energy? If so, it will be healthy for the intrapsychic and relational system.

Does Our Way of Thinking about Problems Contain Inherent Dangers?

I believe that as thinking moved from the supernatural to the Enlightenment, science became entrenched in cause-effect, reductionistic approaches to phenomena. In the industrial era that became the modern age, we have sought to find ultimate answers. This has been exceptionally successful in finding cures for diseases and in explaining most physical processes. However, the approach to uncovering the "truth" has hit some limitations, ushered in by the age of relativity and constructivism culminating in our current era of postmodernism. We have created a world where problems are described and bound in by our language and our explanation. We need to remember that language is a construction (Narrative Model) and that the construction can be useful, but it can also be self-limiting. If we make a diagnosis (DSM-V), the words help to describe and communicate. If we believe these words as absolutes, we will believe in these constructions and look at problems in living as "illness." Viewing problems as illnesses will lead to limited expectations for human potential and deflect our lens from larger contexts that, if addressed, could ameliorate the problem situation.

I call this process the problem box that becomes the box problem. By labeling a process and making it into a static entity, we gain understanding, organize our thinking, and empower our communication. But we lose degrees of freedom for a comprehensive understanding of that problem. A person who is inordinately sad becomes "depressed" (nominalization: the verb becomes a noun). We then may expect less of this person, the person accepts this view of him or herself, and this view perpetuates and confirms the diagnosis. We can lose sight of the multi-determinants of the sadness and of the hope for unburdening this individual and pointing him or her toward health.

I feel that as clinicians we need to know about the Box, but remain outside of it, and, help the client to see that there are ways out. There are choices other than yielding to the constructions. This is the ultimate power of psychotherapy.

Part Five

PUTTING IT ALL TOGETHER

14

A CLOSER LOOK AT TWO APPLICATIONS OF THE INTERNAL FAMILY SYSTEMS METAMODEL

Six-Year-Old Ana and Her Family

Throughout this book, treatment vignettes have been presented in order to highlight the application of the Internal Family Systems MetaModel approach to the healing of children, teens, and their families. In this chapter we can explore in greater depth just how this healing happens. Ana and Blanche did very well in their therapy over a two-year period of time. Let's use a zoom lens to take a closer look at this process with a young child and family.

Blanche was given my name by a relative who is a psychologist and who has been a colleague of mine over the years. This colleague shares my views on a family systems approach to healing child-focused problems. I view it as a courageous act for Blanche to have realized that her own solutions to six-year-old Ana's oppositional behavior were not working. Her request for a referral was a Self-assertive act. She was worn out, anxious, and depressed. She wanted to "get it right" when it came to parenting, and even though she was stretched to the limit in time, energy, and money, she called in the service of helping her daughter.

During the initial phone call Blanche expressed her frustration and became teary when talking about the helplessness of her situation. She was articulate and puzzled as to why the "logical" ways of parenting were not working. I told her that being a single parent in this hyper world is quite a challenge, close to impossible, and that I am not surprised that she feels thwarted and exhausted.

I commended her on calling and asking for help and reassured her that I have helped many families in similar situations. When I asked a bit about the involvement of Ana's father, she told me about his current status of being in a mandated, inpatient drug and alcohol rehab program and that she was livid about his irresponsibility as a parent and did not want him involved in Ana's treatment. I accepted this for the time being and stated that I wanted to continue the conversation about this when we met in person. The beginnings of therapeutic engagement had been established.

Making an appointment for an initial parent consultation meeting was a challenge, given our schedules, but we managed to find an hour to get started.

Blanche arrived for her initial parent consultation meeting after a long day, looking drawn and tired. I began by saying, " Tell me first about the good things in your life." Blanche immediately told me how much she loves Ana and feels like she is a failure as a parent. I slowed her down and said, "We will get to the problem areas, but for now just tell me what's working well." She told me that she loves when she and Ana spend quiet time together at night and cuddle. She feels comforted at those moments. She mentioned that she is well respected in her job as an insurance assessor and has risen through the ranks to a supervisory position. "This is the one thing that my father helped with, getting me the job, as he worked for the same company." She mentioned that her social life is limited, but she has made some friends on the job. She stated that the most soothing moments in her day are after Ana goes to bed and "I can curl up with a good romance novel."

I thanked her for sharing these positives. We then shifted to the challenges in her life. Blanche told me how exasperated she is with Ana's unbounded energy, with Ana moving from activity to activity. This contrasts with Blanche's own low-key energy, such as loving to sit and relax with a good book. She wondered about medication for Ana but does not want to go in that direction. Her pediatrician encouraged her to see what therapy could accomplish. I appreciated that and joined her in that view. I told her that it is difficult to differentiate anxiety from ADHD and temperament, and I would help with sorting this out. Blanche described that Ana's "hissy fits" happened mostly when it was time to be an authoritative parent: getting her up on time, helping her with transitions from one activity to another, or getting her to bed at night. This is when she loses her own temper, yells, and is punitive. "I hate that about myself."

This is where I began to introduce the existence of Parts for Ana and for Blanche: "You appreciate your wonderful daughter and her creativity, but she has a controlling Part that challenges your role as Mom. I see it as my job to get to know Ana's controlling Part and to help it relax over time." Blanche relaxed. The therapist was affirming her daughter's goodness and was expressing curiosity about this Part that they clashed about: "You know, when you call it a controlling Part it doesn't surprise me. Ana has had her young life in a lot of chaos since birth. Why wouldn't she try to get things under control?" I told Blanche that it was great that she can step back from the problem in our session and see it in a new way.

I asked Blanche that while I help Ana with her controlling Part, would she like help with how she reacts to that Part? She said, "I'd want to calm my anger and annoyance." I said to Blanche that she, like me and all folks, also has Parts. "I can help you with that annoyed Part so that your day does not have to be ruined by these clashes with your daughter. Let's try to figure out ways to understand and calm that Part of you." Blanche took a full breath.

The balance of this initial assessment session was taking some family history. Significant to note, Blanche's father was a severe alcoholic and died several years ago from liver failure. She mentioned that he was an unhappy man who was very demanding of her and her sister, but particularly critical of her throughout her life. "He always thought I could be more." Her Mom was a "free spirit" and very self-involved, working full-time and assuming that Blanche would be around to take care of her younger sister, severely limiting Blanche's social life. "I had to grow myself up." We then shifted our discussion to the role of Ana's ex-husband, Charlie, in treatment. Blanche said that she thought about this after our initial phone conversation. Inasmuch as Charlie was going to have regular contact with Ana, who idealizes and also fears him, she thought that he should be involved, but made it clear that she cannot stand him. She had been traumatized by a brief marriage that including alcoholic binges and physical assaults witnessed by Ana. She gave me Charlie's phone number at the rehab center.

Blanche expressed hopefulness, and we set up an appointment for Ana to be seen for assessment. She wasn't sure what Ana would make of therapy and said I should be ready for a "force of nature." I told her that since Ana is six years old, her sessions may be a combination of individual and parent-child segments.

I left a voice-mail message for Charlie in the intervening week.

The next week, I greeted Ana and Blanche in the waiting room. Anna bounded up, dragging her mom with her to the treatment room. I guess I was going to start with mother and daughter together! I welcomed Ana to the office and saw her make a quick and thorough survey of her surroundings. She told me that her mom told her that they were here to "talk about their problems."

I said that we will get to that, but first I wanted to hear about the good things in her life. She told me that she loves school and her teacher. She was making new friends in first grade. (She was quite verbal and used mature language.) She told me that she loves art projects and really likes soccer, "it's fun running all over the field." She told me that she enjoys the weekend visits with her Dad and right now, "he lives in a place to help him feel better and I visit him there."(Blanche gave me a furtive look, as if to say, "Ana doesn't know the full story about this.") She loves the fun times playing with her mom, especially playing doctor to her mom, the patient.

When we shifted to areas of concern, Ana said, "It's my hissy fits. I can't stop them. Mom and me fight about them a lot." Introducing Parts language, I said, "Maybe I need to understand that hissy fit Part of you so we can help it relax a bit." She shook her head in agreement. I asked Ana if it would be okay if we had some time together while her mom sat in the waiting room, and she was fine with this idea.

Ana did some drawing. She is quite skillful at this. During the activity she was calm and quite immersed. The sense was that she felt comfortable with my presence and soothed by the activity. We talked a bit, but this was incidental to the activity. When asked, Ana was very enthusiastic about coming back, wanting her mom to be in a segment of the session, and then having time to play. I agreed to this as it fit for her style and age. When I told her it was time to end our session she ignored me, continuing with her drawing. I waited and stated it again. She said she needed to complete her picture. This placed a pressure on my schedule. My experience of Ana's lingering felt like a combination of an internal need to be soothed by reaching closure on an activity, and an interpersonal assertion of her being in control of the relationship. She finished and ran to the waiting room. We brought Blanche in for a moment. Ana told her that we talked and had fun. She gave her picture to her mom. I got to know Ana in this assessment session. We scheduled another for the following week.

During the next week, Charlie called. I found out that his rehab facility was about two hours away, and he had limited leave and was without a car. We agreed that we would try hard to schedule an appointment, but decided to have a phone session for now since it was a challenge to set up an appointment. He wanted to know what I thought about Ana. I told him that she was a great kid but feeling a lot of anxiety in her life. He agreed, admitting that he was not a great help in this regard. I emphasized his importance to Ana, that I wanted him involved in this treatment, and that this was agreed to by Blanche. He told me that he was working hard to be abstinent of drugs and alcohol and that this stint in rehab (his third mandated treatment) seemed to be helpful. He wanted to be helpful to Ana's treatment and was struggling with whether and how to tell Ana about his addictions. I told him that I'd be glad to guide this process over time. I mentioned that I would be helping to understand the hissy fits and finding a way for this Part of Ana to relax, and that I was available for him to call me with questions. Charlie mentioned that his current marriage was on shaky ground and that his wife adored time with Ana. Also, and quite importantly, his mother was a very devoted grandmother to Ana. We began well and committed to be in contact.

I called Blanche to let her know that contact with Charlie had occurred. She was now supportive of this.

Ana was excited to come for her second assessment session. This time I suggested that we wait for later in the session to have her mom join us, and she was fine with this. She entered the office and said, "I had a big hissy fit this week." I told her that I was glad that she could tell me about this. I asked about good stuff happening. Her teacher told her that she wrote a great story for a school project. I mentioned that I spoke with her dad, and she was very pleased, hoping that he would eventually join her in a session in the future. "I want to show him all the stuff in the office," she replied.

I then asked her to tell me more about the hissy fit Part. "When does it get set off?" Ana thought and said, "When I'm gonna miss my Mom. Like at night when we have to stop playing and its time to go to bed or in the morning when its time to go to school and she goes to work." I said, "So, it's a Part of you that tries to help when you get sad. It tries to get more time with Mom." Ana was quiet and reflective. "Yeah, I guess . . . and it blocks the sad feelings . . . but I hate it, I hate the fights with Mom." I said, "Wow, thanks Ana for being so smart to know all of this. This hissy fit Part works hard, kind of like a control Part for your feelings and your time with Mom, to help you with your sadness but it creates another problem: fights with Mom. Maybe we can find a way to help with the sadness without the fights. Does Mom know about all of this?" Ana replied, "No. Can you tell her when she comes in?"

"Absolutely."

After some drawing on the chalkboard with Ana as the "teacher," we brought Blanche in to the session. Just as Blanche was seated, Ana jumped up and said to her, "My hissy fit Part comes out when I'm sad about you going away." Blanche looked at her, wanting to hear more. "When you go away or I think about your going away, I get sad and then I yell and scream." Blanche got teary and said, "Come here," reaching for Ana to come. She gave Ana a big hug and kiss and held her tight. Ana snuggled into her mom's arms. We all just sat and lingered on this loving, Self-led Part for Blanche understanding the Protective nature of the hissy fits (Manager and Firefighter). We had the expression and experience of the Functional Hypothesis, the protective intent of the troubling symptoms. More than I could verbalize, our assessment, though a bit unorthodox in terms of the five-session sequence spelled out in an earlier chapter, was essentially complete. I thanked mother and daughter for their openness and for being brave enough to allow these feelings to be expressed so lovingly. I invited Blanche in for the next session to officially round out the assessment sessions.

Blanche arrived the next week, looking lighter in her mood. She said that Ana was really trying hard not to have hissy fits. There were fewer outbursts in the past week. I said that this was great to hear about, but also explained that I did not want Ana to be trying so hard to control her outbursts. "We learned that these are important coping Parts and will gradually diminish as the sadness is attended to. She doesn't need to *force* the process."

Blanche was a bit confused about this. I stated that I did not want Ana to try to be in an internal battle with this control Part (in essence, managing a Manager, as this would lead to a internal polarization). "When Ana is unburdened of her sadness, the control Part will feel safe enough to relax on its own. I don't want Ana to have to be a disciplinary Parent to this Part." (This is just what concerns me about cognitive behavioral treatments, that is, imposing constraints on "disordered thoughts" and "irrational feelings." At best, this works in the short term but creates confusion and havoc on the internal emotional system.) Blanche replied, "Hmm . . . not sure I fully get that, but I do see that that style creates a lot of pressure on her."

I asked Blanche how she was doing within herself. She said, definitely more relaxed. "I'm still overwhelmed when Ana's barrage is coming at me, but it's like I don't take it so personally." I expressed delight about this shift. We set up three sessions per month for Ana to be seen individually, with a segment for mother and daughter in the latter part of the session. One session per month was to be a parent session for Blanche.

The next week, Charlie and I were able to meet. I found him to be depressed and down-and-out regarding the shambles of his life—a failed marriage, shame about his violence when drunk, the loss of his job, and his current wife threatening separation and divorce. His love and devotion to Ana were apparent. His inability to reliably parent her added to his shame. He clearly wanted to be helpful regarding Ana's treatment in whatever way he could. Right now he was concentrating on his addictions recovery. I supported the idea to tell Ana in the future about his struggle with alcohol and drugs. I told him my thoughts about the hissy fits. He saw them at times but his blustery style capped them off. He wondered whether his situation was a heavy emotional burden for his daughter and made her sad. I said that it would have to be a part of the picture. We talked about coordinating parental decisions with Blanche. Ana had asked him to come with her to a session. He was agreeable to this. We planned to meet soon, and I told him that I would adjust the fee until he was able to get regular employment. As the session was reaching its end, I said, "Charlie, I appreciate that you came here today. Sorry that your life has been filled with so many struggles. I am available to guide your connection to Ana and to be an additional help to answer any questions that come up during your rehab process." He made eye contact and expressed appreciation for this.

This completed the assessment phase. I have represented in Figure 14.1 how I see the mother-daughter, Parts-to-Parts interaction at the outset between Ana and Blanche. We can see how the Protective Parts of Ana triggered vulnerability and feeling of inadequacy in Blanche and how Blanche's disciplinary reactivity to her daughter triggered sadness and feelings of inadequacy for Ana. This interaction becomes a vicious cycle as long as Self-energy is bypassed and the burdens of Exiles are carried by both. The future of our therapy would need to be (1) diminishing

Ana and Blanche/Part-to-Part Interaction

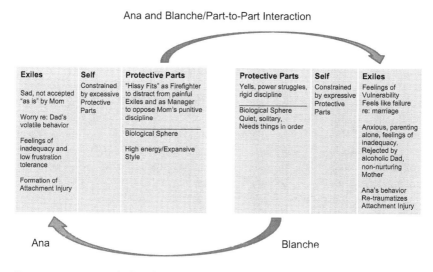

Exiles	Self	Protective Parts		Protective Parts	Self	Exiles
Sad, not accepted "as is" by Mom	Constrained by excessive Protective Parts	"Hissy Fits" as Firefighter to distract from painful Exiles and as Manager to oppose Mom's punitive discipline		Yells, power struggles, rigid discipline	Constrained by expressive Protective Parts	Feelings of Vulnerability Feels like failure re: marriage
Worry re: Dad's volatile behavior				Biological Sphere Quiet, solitary, Needs things in order		
Feelings of inadequacy and low frustration tolerance		Biological Sphere High energy/Expansive Style				Anxious, parenting alone, feelings of inadequacy. Rejected by alcoholic Dad, non-nurturing Mother
Formation of Attachment Injury						Ana's behavior Re-traumatizes Attachment Injury

Ana   Blanche

Figure 14.1 Ana and Blanche/Part-to-Part Interaction

the tenacity of Protective Parts, thereby lifting constraints on Self-energy for both, (2) bringing Self-energy to help unburden the Exiles, and (3) having mother and daughter in a Self-to-Self loving relationship. Involving the father in this process would lead to further unburdening the painful feelings carried by Ana.

We began our ongoing therapy. Ana arrived enthusiastically each week and often was a whirlwind of energy, busying herself in projects and immersing herself in a very focused manner in these activities. She enjoyed filling bowls of water, shaping "sculptures" out of wet paper towels, etc. She often would report on having a good week in school and enjoying her art classes, soccer practice, and games. She would tell me how she was trying not to have hissy fits, but that sometimes this was hard. I told her that the hissy fit Part would relax when the worry/sadness Part of her felt that it was being helped and comforted. She told me that her Mom was trying to spend more time with her and this helped. When asked, Ana continued to tell me that she hated the hissy fit Part. I suggested that we do a relaxation exercise so that we could try to talk to the feelings and Parts inside. She tried this. I began with making Direct Access with the Part that disliked the hissy fit/control Part. I asked if it would be willing to step back so that we could have a clear channel to the hissy fit Part. Ana was compliant, but I did not think that this was making a direct emotional hit to her internal system. She seemed to be "getting it," but on a more cognitive level. Progress leveled off and, at times the hissy fits intensified, leaving Ana and Blanche feeling somewhat defeated. Having seen this trajectory of change many times, I normalized this development and kept trying to reach these Parts via play and discussion. In play, Ana was able to draw (externalize) the hissy fit Part with an aggressive scribble of red and purple colors. We talked to it and about her feelings towards it. At times, this unblending allowed for the entry of worry and sadness (Exiles) to the surface. Ana felt that her family situation was "not normal," living with a single mom and having her dad living at "the center." She carried shame and feelings of "being different" about this.

During a play activity in a session, Ana seemed a bit more edgy than usual. I asked her "What's up?" She pushed me. I asked, "What's going on Ana?" She said she was remembering seeing her dad push her mom like that when she was a very young child. I commented on how scary that had to be for a little kid. "It was scary watching and worrying about Mom. I think it was after that that my father left the house." I lingered on that and appreciated Ana telling me about it. "Yeah, I kept that inside for a long time . . . can't tell Mom, she doesn't want to remember that stuff." I told her that these scary memories are hard for kids, and they take up energy inside them as secrets. "I am glad to know this secret so we can gradually have you let go of this stuff. I may ask your permission to speak to Mom about this at a later time." At a later time, Ana did allow me to tell her mom. I spoke with Blanche, who confirmed the accuracy of this incident and said that there were many such events in those years of the marriage. In a mother-daughter segment, Blanche acknowledged how hard this was for her little girl and told Ana how sorry she was for putting her through this. Ana asked her mom how these memories are for her, and Blanche quietly said that they are painful but it gets easier over time.

Weeks went by. Ana and Blanche were doing better. In one session, Ana expressed resentment to me because our time together, while fun, prevented her from going to a play date with a friend. I accepted these feelings and commended her for being so able to express herself. I told her that she should be doing all the things that kids her age had fun with.

I set up a session for Ana and father. Ana showed her dad around the office and told him about many of the games and projects that we did together. There was a loving bond between them. A bit of awkwardness also existed, as their interaction was often action oriented and busy on weekends, and not really focused on feelings. Ana told her dad that she missed him and thought of him during the week. She also worried about his health since she assumed he was "ill," necessitating his living away. Her dad turned to me and said that he thought he was ready to tell Ana the fuller story about his problem. He asked Ana to sit beside him and told her about his problem with drinking. He said that he was very sorry that he caused Ana so much worry, but he wanted her to know that he was making progress and would soon be back living nearby, finding a job and being with her more. Ana was greatly relieved at this revelation. I greatly appreciated that Charlie was able to express himself so effectively. She leaned her head on his shoulder and said, "I'm glad that you are OK . . . I worry about you."

From this point on, Ana was much lighter in mood and clearly less burdened. We checked in with the worry Part and it said that it was feeling better. The hissy fits were greatly reduced. Ana actually raised the idea of coming to therapy less frequently. I was not fully sure of this idea, but supported her request and again supported her need to feel "normal."

Blanche also supported Ana's tapering of sessions and asked to come more regularly herself. We agreed to twice monthly meetings and began to do a deeper exploration of her emotional system.

Blanche would use the beginning of her sessions to report on the steady progress of Ana. We discussed parenting questions as they arose. She then shifted to talk about her experience in her family of origin. As mentioned, Blanche was a parental child, spending much time alone and bearing much responsibility as the caretaker of her younger sister. Her parents were not reliable figures. It was clear that her Attachment was quite insecure and her belief in the dependability of others was shaky. This childhood pain (Exile) was compounded by her traumatic marriage to Charlie. Blanche oscillated between a supercompetent/Manager Part and a socially reclusive couch potato/Firefighter Part that would get its soothing from withdrawing from the world and at times bingeing on sweets. We got to know these Protective Parts and could clearly see how they buffered her own sadness and worry. Blanche was fairly responsive to going inside to speak directly to these Parts. Cautiously, the Protective Parts stepped back, lifting constraints on Self-Energy, then to be directed, with my guidance, to the Exiles. She bravely attended to the sadness and worry, and these feelings were unburdened.

After several months of this work, Blanche ventured out and agreed to date a man, a friend of a friend. She reported having a wonderful time. This relationship has evolved and it looks like an engagement is being planned. Blanche feels very safe with this man, who seems to "get" her.

He has introduced himself to Ana, who is excited about this development, again stating that this holds the promise of being a "normal" family. "He's very kind to Mom and me. Once in a while when I have a hissy fit, he stays calm and does a project with me and lets Mom calm down."

As this relationship progressed, Blanche alternated between excitement and terror at making an emotional commitment to a man. She came to her sessions in the midst of anxiety attacks several times. We revisited the Protective Parts and Blanche was able to reassure them that even though this is scary and there are no guarantees in intimate relationships, she will be okay going forward with this. The therapy with Blanche continues and it looks like we have a "normal" family for Ana.

It should be noted that this treatment was quite a team approach, as "it takes a village" (Clinton, 1996) to accomplish the healing. Ana and Blanche were the centerpiece. Client factors in healing are the most potent (Duncan, Miller, Wampold, & Hubble, 2010). These clients were courageous and open to the process of change. Their Selves were yearning to come out from behind their tenacious Protective Parts. They allowed the safety and security of the sessions to bring repair to the longstanding Attachment Injury for Blanche and the Attachment Injury in formation for Ana. As this was in process, they became more and more receptive to the healing support and Self-energy of those around them, even those who had contributed to the Attachment Injury. Charlie was involved and participated in an important way. While his life had been difficult, he was committed to provide a secure base for Ana. Very fortunately, Blanche now was dating, and she seemed to have chosen an excellent person with good partner potential and a natural feel for connecting with kids. Also very importantly, Charlie's wife remained a solid figure of constancy for Ana, as did Charlie's Mom and Blanche's Mom. Along the way, I had several telephone conferences with Ana's teachers and school psychologist, who adored her while at the same time often felt exhausted by her demands. They learned how to build on her strengths and to harness her high energy for special assignments in school. They listened to the formulation regarding the IFS MetaModel, and felt that this way of viewing Ana was very helpful for them.

Figure 14.2 shows in graphic form the transformation of Ana and Blanche from a Part-to-Part Interaction to a Self-to-Self interaction, resulting in Attachment repair for both.

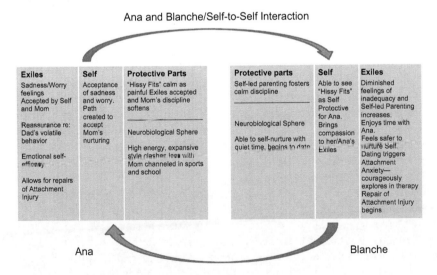

Figure 14.2 Ana and Blanche/Self-to-Self Interaction

Thirteen-Year-Old Drew and His Family

Next, I will present the application of the Internal Family Systems MetaModel to the work I did with an adolescent boy and his family.

Fran called me expressing concern for her thirteen-year-old son, Drew. She was referred to me by a friend whose family had been treated by me in the past. On the phone, she described Drew as being very sullen at home, hardly communicating with her, her husband, Fred, and to Drew's older sister, Ellie. She was worried about his doing minimal schoolwork and his seeming not to care much about things around him. I described the five-session assessment process and expressed confidence that as I get to know Drew and the family I'd be able to be helpful to them. She told me that she wasn't sure whether Drew would come to sessions, and that her husband worked long hours and might not participate. Fran declined my offer to speak with her, her husband, Fred, on the phone and agreed to discuss this process with him and call back to set up an initial parent consultation session. A few days later, Fran called back and the session was arranged.

Fran and Fred arrived in my office and immediately expressed frustration with Drew. I slowed them down a bit and turned to Fred, as I had not had the opportunity to speak with him on the phone. I learned that he worked as a real estate broker for high-end commercial properties and commuted to New York City for long workdays. I sensed a kindness in him, underlying a fast-paced style of talk laced with sarcasm. I asked him about Drew's strengths, and he told me that his son is a talented musician, having learned to play the piano and keyboard, and that Drew was also teaching himself guitar. He identified with this talent, stating that he has a love for music and shyly told me that he would have loved to be a rock musician himself. He also told me that Drew is basically a nice kid with good values, but "he drives me crazy because he seems to be messing up so badly in school and we cannot reach him." He told me that he is upset most of the time in his role of father, as he cannot seem to convince his son to work hard and get the help that he needs. Fran told me how much she cares for Drew, but was extremely frustrated in her attempts to get her son to be more mature and self-reliant in taking care of his responsibilities. Fran is a special education teacher and has had Drew evaluated in school. Fran handed me a ream of reports of evaluations done over several years. Psychological testing indicated a weakness in reading comprehension. Otherwise, Drew tested as average to above average in academic subjects. She also noticed that in school Drew has a very passive attitude in the classroom, seeming to "go through the motions" in his school day. This was in great contrast to his highly animated energy during a recent talent show, in which Drew and his band received much applause from their peers. Fran also mentioned that Drew has had many food and seasonal allergies since birth, including a peanut allergy that twice landed him in the emergency room. He is often physically uncomfortable, with a drippy nose, and very itchy. Fran has spent much time, energy, and money on hiring tutors for Drew, speaking to his teachers, and bringing him to the pediatrician and allergy specialists. Fran said that she feels "on alert" with Drew, vigilant about the next medical emergency or test result in school. She only briefly experienced some "warm and cuddly" time with Drew as an infant. Most of his growing years, she's been "trying to keep him healthy and shape him up."

The parents told me about their 16-year-old daughter, Ellie, who hardly gives Drew "the time of day." She is an extremely diligent student, a perfectionistic in her style, very concerned with her appearance, and worried about fitting in with her peers. She has screamed at her parents many times that all they care about is Drew, while they neglect her needs.

The parents have been married for 21 years. They did not seem to be very supportive of one another, leading more parallel than convergent daily lives. Fred's family of origin are based in Vermont and are only peripherally involved. Fred has an older sister. Fran's parents divorced when she was 12 and both have remarried. They live locally and lend support and connection to their family. Fran is the older of two sisters.

I expressed appreciation for the parents coming in together and giving me such a clear overview of Drew and the family. I told them that I looked forward to meeting Drew and getting to know him. I stated that I was confident that I could help Drew feel better about himself and, if they chose, to also help them feel less burdened by his struggles. Fran asked whether I could help with his learning problems. I replied that I wanted to learn more about this and help reduce the tensions that existed about these problems, and would provide feedback about this at the conclusion of the assessment sessions. When asked, I coached them a bit on preparing Drew for his session, encouraging them to tell him that they were consulting with me in order to help their family relate in a better way.

The following week, I met with Drew. He was a slightly built, pale-looking young man who seemed awkward in his body. He wore a baseball cap in reverse. I reached out to shake his hand and he responded in a weak, passive manner. I welcomed him to the office and asked what he thought about coming in today. He shrugged and said in a mumble, "This is not my idea . . . I'm kind of annoyed with my mother for making me do this . . ." I told him that I appreciated his telling me this and that I could understand his feelings and did not want him to feel forced about being here. Since he *was* here, would it be okay if I found out a bit about him and his life? He mumbled again, "I guess." To which I added, "If there's anything that I ask that you think is a dumb question and you don't want to answer, just tell me and we will skip it." He readily told me that he loves music. I asked him about the kind of music he likes, how he learned to play keyboard and guitar, his band, and so on. This expanded to talking about friends. I learned that he had a few very good friends and that he was very loyal in helping them when they needed him. He never liked sports and felt like an outsider in this area.

When I asked Drew about school, he got quiet. He said that "school sucks, and I'm constantly fighting with my parents about this." I asked if he wanted to talk about this. He shook his head no. I said I totally respected not getting into details about this, but would he mind if I asked some things about the Part of him that hates school. He said, "I'm not sure, but go ahead." I asked him whom he talks to about this Part of him. He replied, "No one." Parents? Friends? "No." "Hmm . . . so you carry these feelings inside you." "I guess." "That's a lot to carry." There was a degree of relaxation in his body posture. I decided that it would be worth a try to probe inside him a bit. "Drew, I know that this school stuff creates a tremendous pressure inside you. I'd like to show you a way to relieve that pressure by going inside yourself with some relaxed breathing, as I guide the process. Willing to try?" "Not sure what this is about, but I'll give it a try." "How do you usually handle something you're not really sure about?" Drew reflected and replied, "I think . . . sometimes I just forget about it and don't do it . . . sometimes I just jump in, like when I snowboard and I see the triple black diamond sign. I just go for it."

"Wow . . . Well, I will be your guide on this trail and will check in with you often to see how you're doing . . . call on me at any point."

I asked Drew to close his eyes and plant his feet on the floor. I first described the healing breath process by taking in breath through the nose, holding it for a moment, and letting it out fully through the mouth. He readily tried it and kept going with just a little prompting. He seemed to welcome this exercise.

Next, I asked, "Drew as you continue to do the breathing, would it be okay if I asked a few questions?" "Okay." "Very good. Drew, see if you can locate inside where this Part is that hates school; where is it in your body?" He took a moment and described tightness in his chest, pressure in his head, and fluttering in his stomach. "That's great that you can tune in to your feelings so well. Drew, when you exhale, take a moment to send some breath to these places in your body that are connected to the Part that hates school." Drew did so, entering fully into this experience. "How is this feeling for you?" "Okay." "Good. Tell me, if you can, how you feel towards this Part that hates school." "I don't like it, that's mainly the pressure in my head that seems to yell and criticize me like my parents." "Wow, amazing that you can identify this. So, Drew, for now, see if you can ask that Part in your head that is critical, if it would be willing to step back so we can focus on the 'I hate school' Part. We can talk to that Part also, but maybe at a later time. Drew was quiet for a few moments. I asked, "How's it going?" "Yeah, it stepped back." "Very good. How do you feel about that Part that hates school now?" "I'm wondering about it . . . how it got so intense." "Very good, so let's be curious about it together. Let's have that Part tell us its story." Drew became self-reflective. "This Part just shuts down about school, tells me to get busy with other things, not do the work, not go to class." "Hmm . . . ask it what it would worry would happen if it didn't work so hard to keep you away from school work." "It doesn't want me to get so frustrated and sad about not being a good reader. It tells me to not do the work so I can avoid those lousy feelings."

I replied, " So, that Part that tells you to not do the school work is actually trying to help you not feel frustrated and sad" (Functional Hypothesis). "Yeah, definitely." "So, Drew, if it makes sense to you, try to thank that Part for working so hard to be of help to you." Drew was quiet for a few moments. His body posture seemed to fold into the couch. I asked, "How is that feeling?" "Amazingly relaxed." "Very good. Drew, ask the Part what it might need from you for it to relax a little bit regarding schoolwork." He took some time considering this idea. "The Part would need to know that I can handle it if I don't understand the schoolwork, and also deal with pressure from my parents and teachers." "Yeah . . . it needs to know that you'll be okay in facing these frustrations. I'm going to be working with your parents to back off on the pressure and, if you give me permission, to speak with your teachers to come up with ideas to help and not push so much. Ask the Part if it could begin to observe that you're doing okay with this and maybe to start to experiment with letting up a bit." More self-reflection. "The Part said that it needs to go slowly with this." I replied, "Yes, absolutely . . . that just shows how devoted it is to protecting you . . . Drew, as you are ready to do so, thank the Part for communicating so well and for its willingness to be helpful. . . . at your own pace, come on out so we can sum up this work."

Drew opened his eyes and smiled, saying, "That was helpful. I get that the 'I hate school' Part is trying to help me." "Yes it is . . . it wants to make sure that you are okay." We talked a bit more, and Drew eagerly agreed to come in for the next assessment session. Drew, while presenting as a withdrawn/avoidant teen wary of adult intervention, when Accepted as he was, and when the Protective Part was unblended from Self, was eager to begin the healing process.

The next day, I received a call from Fran asking how the session with Drew went, as he was silent on the car ride home. I told her that it was a very good beginning, that her son has a lot of strengths, and I was very hopeful about our work together. I told her that it is typical that teens share minimally about their therapy sessions. She expressed her worry about report cards coming out soon and I reminded her that I plan to be helpful to her and Fred in creating a home environment where they are more able to relax about Drew's school achievement.

In the next assessment session, Drew entered the office with eagerness. While maintaining his reserved manner, his gait and energy level were clearly more buoyant. We talked some more about music, with Drew telling me that he was becoming quite savvy about using the computer to enhance his playing and how he was experimenting with writing his own songs. I found this to be quite impressive and my comments, in a natural manner, were celebrating Drew's Self-energy.

He told me that the past week was a good one. He was still struggling with his subjects and told me that his brain feels jumbled when trying to figure out what he is reading. He said that he stopped beating himself up so much about this. I said that that sounded great and wondered what ideas he had about helping the jumbled-up feeling in his brain. "Not sure." I asked if he wanted to go inside again so we could ask about this more directly to the jumbled-up feeling. He very readily said, "Yes."

I asked Drew to begin with breathing as we had done last time. Next, I asked him to contact this jumbled-up feeling in his brain and asked how he felt toward it. "I hate it . . . it's the worst and I feel it all day long in school. I try to get rid of it every day." I said, " Would you want to talk to the Part of you that hates the jumbled-up feeling . . . that critical Part that we said we'd get back to?" "Okay, I'll try." "So, just ask that critical Part to tell you why it puts so much pressure on you." "It's kind of like a force inside me that counters the jumbled-up feeling so that I can get the work done and stay away from the jumbled-up feeling." "Wow, again amazing how your inside Parts are so smart and how, again, we see how the Parts try to help and protect you. So, the critical Part tries to counter the jumbled-up Part and tries to get you to be successful. Let it know that you appreciate its help. Also, let it know that it may be trying so hard and overdoing it and creating so much inside pressure that it ends up backfiring sometimes." "Definitely a lot of pressure that leads me to want to just escape and zone out. My parents don't know but I smoke pot several times a week."

I replied, "Thanks for telling me (Acceptance). You know, it makes sense that when there's a pushy, bossy Part (Manager), there's also a Quick Fix, instant relaxation Part (Firefighter), like smoking pot, to relieve the pressure. They're all working for you . . . we should make a note to try to get to know all of these Parts, so we can get your inner system into a better, healthier balance. That, combined with my working with your parents and teachers to understand and help you better, would be our goal." "Sounds good." Drew was engaged in the healing process and starting to become more clear as to what the possibilities were. Drew came out of the meditative mode, we talked a bit about the experience in the session, and he was pleased. When I inquired, he told me that he was ready for the family session next week.

Drew, in a very insightful manner, had been able to experience and describe his inner landscape of Parts that were currently polarized and stuck on a first-order level of a vicious cycle: The jumbled-up feeling seemed to be a combination of his neurobiological wiring (weakness in reading comprehension) entangled with sadness, and anxiety (Exiles). Two Protective Parts tried to come to the rescue. A critical Part (Manager) that was bossy and obsessive tried to push through the jumbled-up Part so that he could achieve in school. In order to counteract this internal pressure, Drew found pot smoking (Firefighter) was able to relax him and foster an avoidant retreat from responsibilities and the experience of Exiles.

Parents, Drew, and 16-year-old Ellie arrived for the family session. I made a general statement that it was very nice for me to have had the chance to begin to get to know the family and welcomed Ellie, asking her a bit about her school, interests, etc. She answered in a self-assured way and carried a "superior" air about her. The parents stated that they thought their kids were great, but that they felt sad that the family seemed "splintered," with Ellie not home much and very critical of them and Drew. They felt that Ellie was frustrated with Drew for having so many school problems. Fred stated that he thought that Fran treated Drew like a baby and Ellie immediately agreed. Fran could see and even laugh a bit at how she hovered over Drew, but also was annoyed at how Drew's father and sister didn't take Drew's school issues seriously enough. She saw it as her job to prod Drew to do well in school. And she felt alone in that job. Fred agreed with Fran, while Ellie chimed in with, "No one ever helped me." I noted Ellie's frustration and maybe even feelings of being left out, which were "difficult feelings to have." I turned to Drew and asked what he was thinking as he was the subject of the conversation. "This is what goes on every day." "How do you handle this?" "I leave, either literally go to a friend's house or leave in my head by playing music and stuff like that." I asked the parents what they would worry would happen if they stopped trying to manage Drew's schoolwork so much. Fran said that that would be a disaster, fearing that Drew would fail all his subjects. Fred said he wasn't sure Drew could do any worse than he was already doing in school, but that there had to be rules and that his job as a father was to enforce those rules. Ellie said that Drew, like all kids, needed to do his best and handle the consequences if he failed. It became clear that Drew was on the receiving end of a lot of Manager energy from the family. He tried to separate from this external pressure much as he did from his internal pressure. He was engaged in emotional survival strategies.

I mentioned to the family how hard everyone was working to help Drew do better in school. Each of them had a Part that was trying hard to "shape up" Drew. This was a sign of their caring very much, but it did not seem to be working. I asked if Drew could tell his parents and sister how it made him feel when they try so hard to push him to do his schoolwork. Drew hesitated, then said, "It makes me feel like crap. The message that I get is that you think I'm dumb and can't handle the work. I already feel lousy about school. You make me feel even worse." His father said, "We don't want you to fail." His mother said, "It's too much for me when you struggle. I have to do something . . . can't just sit by and watch you struggle." Ellie said, "What's wrong with struggling? That's what life is, especially at this age." Drew looked up and said quietly, "Just leave me alone, I'll be all right." Fran teared up. So did Drew, trying to mask it.

I said to the family that I saw how much they cared for each other. The protection was great, but it might be getting in the way of Drew's growing up. He would need space to trip and fall and to be able to figure out how to pick himself up and handle things. I thanked them for being so brave and so open. I set an appointment for the parents' feedback session.

The parents' feedback session rounded out the assessment phase. The parents told me that the family session was hard, but helpful. The focus was still on Drew, but the conversation shifted a bit to the parents' feelings. Fran said, "I hear what you're saying about my backing off from hovering over Drew, but it's not easy. There's this deep fear inside me that makes this feel dangerous. So when you tell me to back off, I feel like *I'm the failure!*" I told Fran, "I know that this is not easy," and apologized if I did not communicate this to her previously. "How would it be if, as I continue to help Drew deal with his struggles, I try to help you with your frustrations and this feeling about change being dangerous?" She agreed. Fred was supportive and stated that looking at feelings is not his style, so he would be willing to come in periodically, but for now did not want to look inside himself. Fran tried to prod him a bit, and I encouraged her to accept that this is where Fred is for now. I let him know that I was here for the whole family.

I summed up the learning from the assessment sessions: "Drew has a weakness in the area of reading comprehension. This is a disappointment for him. This is compounded by seeing how well Ellie does in this area. You offer lots of help, from your love for him, but this ends up feeling for him like a disapproval, and this started when he was very young, that you are not accepting him as is, that you want him to be different, better. So, the help backfires, and as your very intelligent son said to us, 'makes him feel worse.' Drew has a Part that tries hard for a while and then feels thwarted. After a while another Part of him just decides that it's best to avoid schoolwork altogether. That's especially hard for parents to see. It's the sad Part of him that needs our attention and understanding. That's what I can help him with. And, by the way, that's what you can help him with. This is a very loving family. We need to harness that energy to do some healing." This was the Functional Hypothesis, so far, for this

Drew and Fran/Part-to-Part Interaction

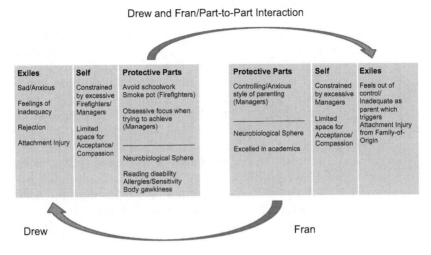

Figure 14.3 Drew and Fran/Part-to-Part Interaction

family. We had placed the presenting symptom, Drew's avoidance of schoolwork, in the emotional context of psychological survival in this family system.

We set up a series of sessions for Drew to come to therapy weekly and Fran, joined by Fred when possible, to have sessions to help the parents with the Parts reactive to stepping back from managing Drew's behavior. We would schedule full-family sessions as needed.

The sessions proceeded. Drew continued to struggle with school but clearly was more accepting of the Part of him that had the learning difficulty. His eagerness for treatment allowed us to bring forward the jumbled-up Part. When he located the jumbled-up Part in his head, he described getting "blurry and foggy," trying to understand what he was reading. The more he forced himself to concentrate, the more foggy he got. I asked him, "Even though it's hard to be in that place, can you bring in that blurry/foggy feeling and just be with it in our session together." He became very quiet and then got very teary. "I just can't do it, I can't understand no matter how hard I try." "Drew, see if you can ask the frustration and anger at yourself to step back."

"Okay." "What's there now?" "Sad, very sad . . . there's something wrong with me." "Hmmm . . . Drew, see if you can bring your caring and compassion to the sadness, just take care of it like it's a good friend." (Pause. Quiet.) "It likes when I'm friendly to it. . . . relaxing . . . smiling . . . sorry that I give you such a hard time. . . . I want to be your friend (big, full breath)." I tell him just to linger exactly where he is. After another pause he said, "I'm okay now." Unburdening had begun. He

136

opened his eyes with an appreciative smile. We talked about re-visiting this Part on his own.

Fran came to the next parent meeting by herself, as was anticipated. She was very impressed with Drew's progress and devotion to figuring things out for himself. It still "drove her crazy" that he put his school-work as a low priority, but she saw him struggling less within himself. She reported that things at home were less stressful. "We know where we are located emotionally. There is less blame, more of a way of looking at each other with a feeling of . . . that's who he is or that's who she is . . ." She reported that Fred was softer with her and Drew. Although Fred rarely talked about his feelings, he seemed less depressed regarding his work and actually signed up for some music lessons and purchased tick-ets for concerts for them to attend as a couple. She mentioned that Ellie actually was seeming to be a worry with her constant striving to be so very perfect. Fran said that she'd like to do some work in therapy to fur-ther ease her controlling and worrying style.

I invited Fran to do some "guided meditation" as an introduction to IFS. She was hesitant but clearly curious. I guided her to focus on her breathing and to use her breath to separate her Self from the long list of responsibili-ties that's constantly on her mind (unblending). "Just linger awhile, expe-riencing you (Self) as separate from all that you do. . . ." Next, I asked if she wanted to help the worry Part. She said, "Definitely yes."

I asked her to locate the worry Part, which she quickly described as being in her head and upper chest. When asked, she said that it felt like a weight that she could not get rid of. I told her that it might be helpful to find more about what this weight is so we could understand it better and be able to help it. I said, "Ask the Part that wants to get rid of the worry Part to step back. Let's create a clear channel between You (Self) and the worry Part. Use your breath to guide this process." Fran worked very quietly, giving a nod here and there. I asked how she now felt toward the worry Part and she said that she was curious about it (a clear enough channel for Self to attend to the Part).

I suggested, "Ask the worry Part to tell you about itself." After a pause, she said, "The worry Part has been with me for a long, long time. It keeps me strong and prepared . . . so I'm always ready for the bad things that can happen. This goes way back to when I was young. My parents were constantly fighting, on the verge of splitting up, which happened when I was 12. The worry kept me ready, on guard (tears). I needed to pro-tect myself from disaster and also help my little sister, who was timid, very scared all the time. . . . It's funny but I feel like I'm back there now, in my room by myself, with the worry. In a funny way, it protected me. It works too hard, is *overprotective,* so my family sees me like I'm an ogre and friends view me as a downer." I said, "Yes, it protected you, prepared you for the worst, the worry Part tries to help you (Functional

Hypothesis) . . . but it overdoes it and can create new problems, especially in your relationships. Just stay in that moment here, in this safe place." Fran's breathing became more fluid, her body more relaxed. After a long pause, I asked, "How is that feeling?" "Great, it's a relief." I said, "If it feels right for you, thank the worry Part for its help in protecting you through all these years. It's been so devoted to you." Fran took some time inside to bring this feeling of gratitude to this Part. "Fran, ask the worry Part if it would be willing to experiment in your daily life with stepping back a bit to see that you can handle things and relate to others without it's being out front in everything that you do." She sensed that it was ready to do this, but it wasn't sure it would be so easy. I said, "Yes, the worry Part is worried for you, doing its job." She laughed and said, "But it seems willing to try."

In future sessions, Fran reported a lifting of the weight of the worry Part that now experienced the grown-up Fran as competent and able to handle life's curves as they inevitably came to be. Fran went inside to contact the sadness (Exiles) that she carried regarding her parents' divorce and the loss of the opportunity for a full, vibrant adolescence. She made the observation that her sad adolescent Part was like a cloud influencing her reactions to her adolescent children. She reported that her relating, in general, was calmer, coming from a more centered place.

Drew continued his sessions. He became immersed in his music, managed to pass his courses, even liked a science or history class here and there. We spent some time talking about pot smoking and saw it as a Firefighter, providing relief from anxiety. He appreciated my not pressuring him about this (the need to calm my own Managers). Drew himself thought it might be a good idea to have a tutor who could guide him with schoolwork. His parents were happy to provide this, which helped to keep them in a more relaxed state as well. Drew used this resource quite well.

Several months later, Ellie asked Fran to call to set up an appointment for her. I discussed this with Drew, who responded with, "She could use some calming down inside her." We talked a bit about the enormous pressure that she puts on herself to achieve. She disclosed that she worries a lot about her attractiveness and how she obsesses about what her peers think about her. She thought that she'd like to be in therapy with a female therapist. I fully supported that request and gave her a referral.

I treated Drew and Fran regularly for several more months. In addition, we had several parent sessions for Fran and Fred. The family was in a better place, navigating the usual bumpy road of life as their kids were growing, and individuating as parents, redefining their vision for new chapters to come. Fred took great delight in Drew's musical pursuits, conversing enthusiastically with his son about this. There was clearly a Self-to-Self connection building in this arena.

At their request, we ended the therapy for the time being. The family was comfortably aware of my being there for them, should the need arise. I asked them to keep in touch, especially to tell me the good things that were going on in their lives.

Over the next few years, I received periodic calls from Fran. I saw the calls as a need for reassurance as challenging life events occurred. Fran's mother was quite ill. She came in for a few sessions to gain some perspective and sort through her deep sadness about this. The family was in a healthier place. As Drew entered his senior year of high school, faced with the pressures of college admission, dating possibilities, etc. he called for a "tune-up." It was wonderful to see him. He was navigating well, also seeking reassurance and further help with his worry Part. We did further work on his feelings of vulnerability, particularly his being non-athletic and awkward and sickly as a young kid.

This led to a discussion of anxieties currently regarding school success. Drew also wanted to talk about his awkwardness regarding dating girls. In this phase of treatment Drew was able to go inside as I guided him to work with his polarized Parts. As he located his obsessional Part and his avoidant Part, I suggested that he invite them into a comfortable room together with Self, unblended, as the chair of the meeting. I asked him to have the Parts make eye contact (or "I" contact, able to bring their good intentions to the meeting and to each other). The Parts listened to each other make a case for the protection of Drew. Self acknowledged this and

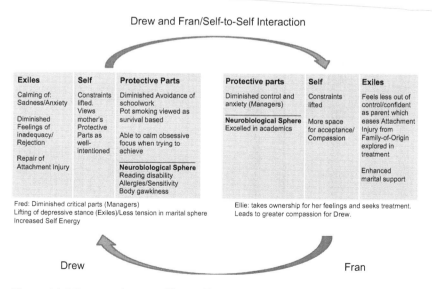

Figure 14.4 Drew and Fran/Self-to-Self Interaction

then was asked to take the leadership position of bringing calmness, clarity, and compassion to his worry and awkwardness (Exiles). The Protective Parts calmed, appreciating this leadership (ultimately what Protective Parts are hoping for). Drew did this with full involvement and reported that it was quite helpful in moving these concerns to a better emotional balance.

He had grown more fully into his body, enjoyed working out, and was thinking of music as a major and possible career. He began dating and was very excited about this. I was delighted to see a wonderful young man ready to launch into the world.

Part Six

CONCLUSIONS AND REFLECTIONS

15

THE REAL PICTURE

I have tried to write this book, sentence by sentence, page by page, in an honest, open-minded and open-hearted manner. What is difficult to describe in words but needs to be said is that psychotherapy is much more than what words can express. It has been an honor for me to work with hundreds of children and their families over my long career. I have written this book with the hope of coaching other therapists in the essence of healing kids and their parents. The process of healing, I feel, is well represented here, yet healing is often experienced through quiet moments of "just being" with a child, matching my breath with his or hers and providing an encouraging voice. Sometimes a gentle pat on the shoulder in support and appreciation of the child is more powerful than any word, than any formalized model.

I refer the reader back to the discussion of KTBB, "kiss the boo-boo." Kids learn affect regulation via Attachments that are safe, secure, and reliable. Being soothed when in distress allows them to feel that the world is a safe place, even when bad things happen. Therapists are uniquely in the role of soothers and comforters. When therapy is successful, youngsters becomes more capable and free to Self-regulate and soothe themselves. All this, of course, applies to the Exiles within parents as well.

As mentioned in the opening pages of this book, all who enter our offices are looking for healing.

We offer Acceptance in a loving setting. Some call this a placebo and try to "control" for this element in research done on psychotherapy. I would say that this "placebo effect" is ultimately the vehicle for emotional healing.

We are not technicians. I believe that the IFS MetaModel model offers the most thorough and most effective process in allowing us to know where we are located at any given moment in our sessions. Are we dealing with a Protective Part? If so, what is the Part trying to help with in the service of the client's survival (Functional Hypothesis)? By befriending the Part we form a healing alliance. Are we in the presence of an Exile? Can we help guide the client's Self (accompanied by our healing Self) to approach, accept, and unburden emotional pain that has been carried for a long time? No, we are not technicians. Our MetaModel provides the words and music from which we need to add harmony, color, and improvisation to make the true artistry of our work come alive.

Therapists will ideally be great listeners to their clients and to their own internal cognitive-emotional system. Some of the most important therapeutic moments are when we are thrown off track from our centered, Self-led position, as a Protective Part of our own is triggered by an extreme Part of the client. Self-care for this event is crucial so that we can return to center and be helpful to the client. Self-care will include momentary reassurance that we are dealing with the residue of the client's history of trauma and to spend time at some point later in the day to be quiet and go inside to see what our activated, agitated Parts need from our Self. The MetaModel serves powerfully as a map for healing via our own clarity.

In this way, IFS is our GPS. When we know where we are located, we can guide children and families in Self-led directions. We bring our empathy, filled with caring, compassion, creativity, and courage and travel together.

Enjoy many safe and meaningful journeys.

REFERENCES AND
FURTHER READING

All authors create new ideas from a solid foundation built by predecessors. The following list of gems is the foundation I stand on quite proudly. I hope that these readings will serve others, as they have provided for me a fuller understanding of the essence of human nature and emotional healing.

Adler, A. (1927). *The practice and theory of individual psychology.* New York: Harcourt, Brace & World.

Anderson, H. (1995). *Conversation, language and possibilities.* New York, NY: Basic Books.

Angier, N. (December 24, 1991). Biologists advise doctors to think like Darwin. *The New York Times, Science Times,* C1.

Bach, P. A., & Moran, D. J. (2008). *ACT in clinical practice: Case conceptualization in acceptance & commitment therapy.* Oakland, CA: New Harbinger.

Bandler, R., & Grinder, J. (1975). *The structure of magic* (Vols. 1–2). Palo Alto, CA: Science and Behavior Books.

Bandura, A. (1977). Self efficacy: Toward a unifying theory of behavior change. *Psychological Review, 84*(2), 191–215.

Bank, S., & Kahn, M. (1982). *The sibling bond.* New York, NY: Basic Books.

Barkley, R. A. (1987). *Defiant children: A clinician's manual for parent training.* New York, NY: Guilford Press.

Bateson, G. (1972). *Steps to an ecology of mind.* New York, NY: Ballantine Books.

Bateson, G. (1979). *Mind and nature.* New York, NY: Bantam Books.

Bateson, G., Jackson, D., Haley, J., & Weakland, J. (1956/1981). Toward a theory of schizophrenia. In R. J. Green & J. L. Framo (Eds.), *Family therapy: Major contributions* (pp. 41–68). New York, NY: International University Press.

Becker, E. (1973). *The denial of death.* New York, NY: Free Press

Bowen, M. (1978). *Family therapy in clinical practice.* New York, NY: Aronson.

Bowlby, J. (1973). *Separation: Anxiety and anger.* New York, NY: Basic Books.

Breunlin, D. (1999). Toward a theory of constraints. *Journal of Marital and Family Therapy, 25,* 365–382.

Breunlin, D., Schwartz, R., & MacKune-Karrer, B. (1992). *Metaframeworks: Transcending models of family therapy.* San Francisco, CA: Jossey-Bass.

Bromberg, P. M. (2006). *Awakening the dreamer: Clinical journeys.* New York, NY: Taylor and Francis.

Carter, B., & McGoldrick, M. (Eds.) (1989). *The changing family life cycle.* Boston, MA: Allyn & Bacon.

Castonguay, L. G., & Hill, C. E. (2007). *Insight in psychotherapy.* Washington, DC: American Psychological Association.

Chess, S., Thomas, A., & Birch, H. G. (1968). *Temperament and behavior disorders in children.* New York: International Universities Press.

Clinton, H. (1996). *It takes a village.* New York, NY: Simon & Schuster.

Courtois, C. (1988). *Healing the incest wound: Adult survivors in therapy.* New York, NY: Norton.

Dadds, M. (1987). Families and the origin of child behavior problems. *Family Process, 26,* 341–357.

Darwin, C. (1859). *On the origin of species.* London: Murray.

Darwin, C. (1871). *The descent of man.* London: Murray.

Dell, P. (1986). Why do we still call them paradoxes? *Family Process, 25,* 223–233.

De Shazer, S. (1982). *Patterns of brief family therapy: An ecosystem approach.* New York, NY: Guilford.

Duncan, B. L., Miller, S. D., Wampold, B. E., & Hubble, M. A. (Eds.) (2010). *The heart and soul of change: Delivering what works in therapy* (2nd Ed.). Washington, DC: American Psychological Association.

Dunn, J., & Plomin, R. (1990). *Separate lives: Why siblings are so different.* New York, NY: Basic Books.

Erickson, M. H. (1962). The identification of a secure reality. *Family Process, 1,* 294–303.

Fishbane, M. D. (2008). "News from neuroscience.": Applications to couples therapy [Monograph]. *AFTA, Winter 2008, 20*–28.

Forehand, R., & McMahon, R. (1981). *Helping the noncompliant child: A clinician's guide to parent training.* New York, NY: Guilford Press.

Frank, J. D., & Frank, J. B. (1991). *Persuasion and healing.* Baltimore, MD: Johns Hopkins University Press.

Fraser, J. S., & Solovey, A. D. (2007). *Second-order change in psychotherapy: The golden thread that unifies effective treatments.* Washington, DC: American Psychological Association.

Gardner, R. A. (1976). *Psychotherapeutic approaches to the resistant child.* New York, NY: Jason Aronson.

Garfield, S. (1992). Eclectic psychotherapy: A common factors approach. In J. C. Norcross & M. R. Goldfried (Eds.), *Handbook of psychotherapy integration* (pp. 169–201). New York, NY: Basic Books.

Gergen, K. J. (2002). Psychological science in a postmodern context. *American Psychologist, 56*(10), 803–819.

Gold, J. (2006). Patient-initiated integration. In G. Stricker & J. Gold (Eds.), *A casebook of psychotherapy integration* (pp. 253–260). Washington, DC: American Psychological Association.

Goldner, V. A. (1985). Feminism and family therapy. *Family Process, 24,* 31–47.

Goldner, V. A. (1998). The treatment of violence and victimization in intimate relationships. *Family Process, 37,* 263–286.

Greco, L. A., & Hayes, S. C. (2008). *Acceptance & mindfulness treatment for children & adolescents: A practitioner's guide.* Oakland, CA: New Harbinger.

Greenberg, L., & Johnson, A. (1988). *Emotionally focused therapy for couples.* New York, NY: Guilford.

Guerin, P. (1976). *Family therapy.* New York, NY: Gardner.

Guerin, P., Fay, L., Burden, S., & Kautto, J. (1987). *The evaluation and treatment of marital conflict.* New York: Basic Books.

Guerin, P., Fogarty, T., Fay, L., & Kautto, J. G. (1996). *Working with relationship triangles: The one-two-three of psychotherapy.* New York, NY: Guilford Press.

Haley, J. (1973). *Uncommon therapy.* New York, NY: Norton.

Haley, J. (1980). *Leaving home.* New York, NY: McGraw-Hill.

Haley, J. (1981). *Reflections on therapy and other essays.* Chevy Chase, MD: The Family Therapy Institute.

Haley, J. (1987). *Problem-solving therapy* (2nd Ed.). San Francisco, CA: Jossey-Bass.

Hare-Mustin, R. T., & Maracek, J. (Eds.). (1990). *Making a difference: Psychology and the construction of gender.* New Haven, CT: Yale University Press.

Hayes, S. C., Strosahl, K. D., & Wilson, K. G. (1999). *Acceptance and commitment therapy: An experiential approach to behavior change.* New York, NY: Guilford.

Herman, J. (1992). *Trauma and recovery.* New York, NY: Basic Books.

Horne, A. M., & Sayger, T. V. (1990). *Treating conduct and oppositional defiant disorders in children.* New York, NY: Pergamon Press.

Hubble, M., Duncan, B., & Miller, S. (Eds.) (1999). *The heart and soul of change: What works in therapy.* Washington, DC: American Psychological Association.

Jacobson, N. S., & Christiansen, A. (1996). *Integrative couple therapy.* New York, NY: Norton.

Johnson, S. (2004). *The practice of emotionally focused couple therapy.* New York, NY: Brunner-Routledge.

Johnson, S., & Whiffen, V. (Eds.) (2003). *Attachment processes in couple and family therapy.* New York, NY: Guilford.

Kerr, M. E., & Bowen, M. (1988). *Family evaluation: An approach based on Bowen theory.* New York, NY: Norton.

Kim, S., Polman, E., & Sanchez-Burks, J. (2012, February 26). When truisms are true. *New York Times, Sunday Review,* p. 12.

Krause, P. K. (2013). IFS with children and adolescents. In M. Sweezy & L. Ziskind (Eds.), *Internal family systems therapy: New dimensions* (pp. 35–54). New York, NY: Routledge.

Kuhn, T. (1962). *The structure of scientific revolutions.* Chicago, IL: University of Chicago Press.

Linehan, M. M. (1993). *Cognitive-behavioral therapy for borderline personality disorder.* New York, NY: Guilford Press.

Luborsky, L. (1995). Are common factors across different psychotherapies the main explanation of the Dodo bird verdict that "everyone has won so all must have prizes"? *Clinical Psychology: Science and Practice, 2,* 106–109.

Luborsky, L., Singer, B., & Luborsky, L. (1975). Comparative studies of psychotherapies: Is it true that "Everyone has won and all must have prizes"? *Archives of General Psychiatry, 32,* 995–1008.

Mahler, M., Pine, F., & Bergman, A. (1975). *The psychological birth of the human infant: Symbiosis and individuation.* New York, NY: Basic Books.

Mahoney, M. (2003). *Constructive psychotherapy: A practical guide.* New York, NY: Guilford.

Marra, T. (2005). *Dialectical behavior therapy in private practice: A practical & comprehensive guide.* Oakland, CA: New Harbinger.

Masterson, J. (1976). *Psychotherapy of the borderline adult: A developmental approach.* New York, NY: Bruner/Mazel.

Mayr, E. (2001). *What evolution is.* New York, NY: Basic Books.

McConnell, S. (2013). Somatic IFS Therapy. In M. Sweezy & L. Ziskind (Eds.), *Internal family systems therapy: New dimensions* (pp. 90–106). New York, NY: Routledge.

McGoldrick, M. (2008). *Genograms: Assessment and intervention* (3rd Ed.). New York, NY: Norton.

McGoldrick, M., Pearce, J. K., & Giordano, J. (Eds.) (1982). *Ethnicity and family therapy.* New York, NY: Guilford.

Mikesell, R. H., Lusterman, D., & McDaniel, S. H., (Eds.) (1995). *Integrating family therapy: Handbook of family psychology and systems theory.* Washington, DC: American Psychological Association.

Minuchin, S. (1974). *Families and family therapy.* Cambridge, MA: Harvard University Press.

Minuchin, S., & Fishman, H. (1981). *Family therapy techniques.* Cambridge, MA: Harvard University Press.

Minuchin, S., & Elizur, J. (1989). *Institutionalizing madness.* New York: Basic Books.

Mones, A. (1998a). Oppositional children and their families: An adaptational dance in space and time. *American Journal of Orthopsychiatry, 68,* 147–153.

Mones, A. (1998b). Oppositional behavior in children. In R. A. Javier & W. G. Herron (Eds.), *Personality development and psychotherapy in our diverse society,* pp. 258–281.

Mones, A. (2001). Exploring themes of sibling experience to help resolve couples conflict. *The Family Journal: Counseling and Therapy for Couples and Families, 9*(4), 455–460.

Mones, A. (2003). The (r)evolution of family therapy: Adaptation, protection and the functional hypothesis from Bateson to internal family systems therapy. *Journal of Self Leadership, 1,* pp. 9–14.

Mones, A., & Panitz, P. (1994). Marital violence: An integrated systems approach. *Journal of Social Distress and the Homeless, 3*(1), pp. 39–51.

Mones, A., & Patalano, F. (2000). From projective identification to empathic connection: The transformation of a marriage from the inside out. *Journal of Couples Therapy, 9,* 57–66.

Mones, A., & Schwartz, R. C. (2007). The functional hypothesis: A family systems contribution toward an understanding of the healing process of the common factors. *Journal of Psychotherapy Integration, 17*(4), 314–329.

Nichols, M., & Schwartz, R. C. (Eds.) (2004). *Family therapy: Concepts and methods.* Boston, MA: Allyn & Bacon.

Niebhur, R. (circa 1937). "The Serenity Prayer." In *The big book (2001).* Alcoholics Anonymous World Services.

Ogden, P., Minton, K., & Pain, C. (2006). *Trauma and the body: A sensorimotor approach.* New York, NY: Norton.

Palazolli, M. S., Cecchin, G., & Boscolo, L. (1978). *Paradox and counterparadox: A new model in the therapy of the family in schizophrenic transition*. New York, NY: Jason Aronson.

Patterson, G. (1982). *Coercive family process*. Eugene, OR: Catalia Press.

Pert, C. (1997). *Molecules of emotion*. New York, NY: Touchstone Books.

Piaget, J. (1962). *The moral judgement of the child*. London: Kegan Paul.

Pinsof, W. (1995). *Integrative problem centered therapy: Family systems, individual and biological theories*. New York, NY: Basic Books.

Porges, S. (2011). *The polyvagal theory: Neurophysiological foundations of emotions, attachment, connection and self regulation*. New York, NY: Norton.

Prochaska, J., & DiClemente, C. C. (1984). *A transtheoretical approach: Crossing traditional lines of therapy*. Homewood, IL: Dorsey.

Roffman, A. (2005). Function at the junction: Revisiting the idea of functionality in family therapy. *Journal of Marital and Family Therapy, 31*, 259–268.

Rosenzweig, S. (1936). Some implicit common factors in diverse methods of psychotherapy. *Journal of Orthopsychiatry, 6*, 412–415.

Rossi, E. L., & Ryan, M. O. (1992). *The seminars, workshops and lectures of Milton H. Erickson: Mind-body communication in hypnosis* (Vol. 3). New York, NY: Irvington.

Rothschild, B. (2000). *The body remembers*. New York, NY: Norton.

Scheinkman, M. & Fishbane, M. (2004). The vulnerability cycle: Working with impasses in couple therapy. *Family Process, 43*, 279–298.

Schwartz, R. C. (1995). *Internal family systems therapy*. New York, NY: Guilford.

Schwartz, R. C. (2001). *Introduction to the internal family systems model*. Oak Park, IL: Center for Self Leadership.

Schwartz, R. C., & Goulding, R. (1995). *The mosaic mind: empowering the tormented selves of child abuse survivors*. New York, NY: Norton.

Scovern, A. (1999). From placebo to alliance: The role of common factors in medicine. In M. Hubble, B. Duncan, & S. Miller (Eds.), *The heart and soul of change: What works in therapy* (pp. 259–295). Washington, DC: American Psychological Association.

Selye, H. (1956). *The stress of life*. New York, NY: McGraw-Hill.

Sherman, R., & Dinkmeyer, D. (1987). *Systems of family therapy: An Adlerian integration*. New York, NY: Brunner/Mazel.

Siegel, D. (1999). *The developing mind: How relationships and the brain interact to shape who we are*. New York, NY: Guilford.

Sprintzen, D. (2009). *Critique of western philosophy and social theory*. New York: Palgrave Macmillan.

Stern, M. B. (2002). *Child-friendly therapy: Biopsychosocial innovations for children & families*. New York, NY: Norton.

Stricker, G. (1994). Reflections on psychotherapy integration. *Clinical Psychology: Science and Practice, 1*, 3–12.

Stricker, G., & Gold, J. (Eds.) (2006). *A casebook of psychotherapy integration*. Washington, DC: American Psychological Association.

Sulloway, F. (1996). *Born to rebel*. New York, NY: Pantheon.

Taffel, R. (2001). *The second family: How adolescent power is challenging the American family*. New York: St. Martin's Press.

Taffel, R. (2005). *Breaking through to teens*. New York: Guilford.

Tolle, E. (2005). *A new earth: Awakening to your life's purpose*. New York, NY: Penguin.

Toman, W. (1976). *Family constellation* (3rd Ed.). New York, NY: Springer

Toman, W. (1988). *Family therapy and sibling position*. Northvale, NJ: Jason Aronson.

Turecki, S. (with Tonner, L.). (1985). *The difficult child*. New York, NY: Bantam.

van der Kolk, B. (1987). *Psychological trauma*. Washington, DC: American Psychiatric Press.

van der Kolk, B. P. Ogden, K. Minton, & C. Pain, (2006). *Introduction, Trauma and the body: A sensorimotor approach* (pp. xvii–xxvi). New York, NY: Norton.

Wachtel, E. (1994). *Treating troubled children and their families*. New York, NY: Guilford.

Wachtel, P. (1977). *Psychoanalysis and behavior therapy: Toward an integration*. New York, NY: Basic Books.

Wachtel, P. (2011). *Inside the session: What really happens in psychotherapy*. Washington, DC: American Psychological Association.

Wampold, B. E. (2001). *The great psychotherapy debate: Models, methods and findings*. New York, NY: Routledge.

Wampold, B. E. (2010). The research evidence for the common factors models: A historically situated perspective. In B. L. Duncan, S. D. Miller, B. E. Wampold & M. A. Hubble (Eds.), *The heart and soul of change: Delivering what works in therapy* (2nd Ed.) (pp. 49–81). Washington, DC: American Psychological Association.

Watzlawick, P., Weakland, J., & Fisch, R. (1974). *Change: Principles of problem formation and problem resolution*. New York, NY: Norton.

Webster-Stratton, C., & Herbert, M. (1994). *Troubled families/problem children*. New York, NY: Wiley.

White, M., & Epston, D. (1990). *Narrative means to therapeutic ends*. New York, NY: Norton.

INDEX